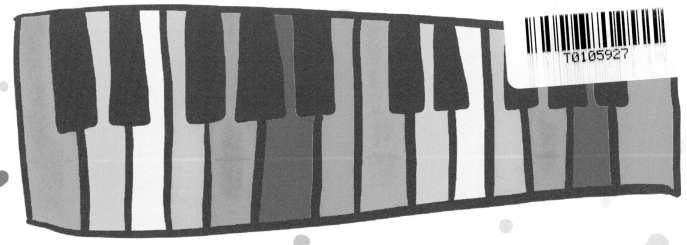

VISUALIZE KEYBOARD
SCALES & MODES

organized by tonic

FOR ALL MUSICIANS

MALIA JADE ROBERSON, PH.D.

ISBN 978-1-5400-8788-1

HAL•LEONARD®

Visit Hal Leonard Online at
www.halleonard.com

Contact us:
Hal Leonard
7777 West Bluemound Road
Milwaukee, WI 53213
Email: info@halleonard.com

In Europe, contact:
Hal Leonard Europe Limited
42 Wigmore Street
Marylebone, London, W1U 2RN
Email: info@halleonardeurope.com

In Australia, contact:
Hal Leonard Australia Pty. Ltd.
4 Lentara Court
Cheltenham, Victoria, 3192 Australia
Email: info@halleonard.com.au

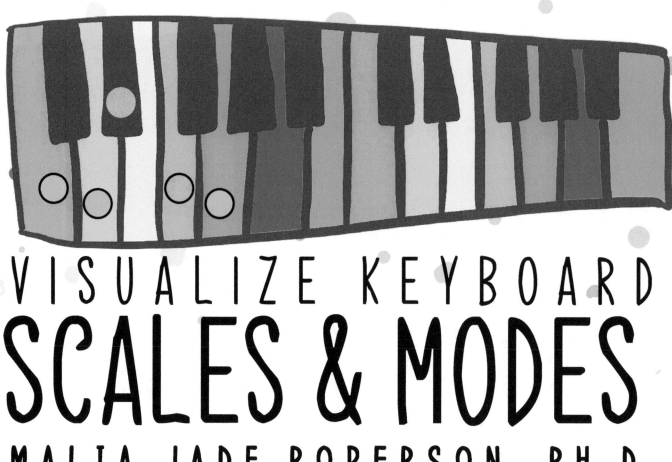

VISUALIZE KEYBOARD
SCALES & MODES
MALIA JADE ROBERSON, PH.D.

Editor, Dr. Irene Montefiore Girton, *Occidental College*
Music Editor, Matt Wolf, *Hal Leonard LLC*

Acknowledgements

Special thanks to Dr. Russ Knight, College of the Desert, and Dr. Pieter van den Toorn, University of California, Santa Barbara, for their insightful feedback and reviews.

Thank you, Society for Music Theory Workshops in Music Theory Pedagogy (2019) at the University of Massachusetts, Amherst, and the Pedagogy into Practice Conference (2019) at the University of California, Santa Barbara. These events deeply influenced the development of this book and inspired me to create, and to continue creating, equitable learning tools for musicians. Thank you, California State University, Channel Islands, for providing me the opportunity to participate in both events.

Thank you, Mom, Dad, Grandma, Shala, Noah, Brooklynn, Harley, & Cooper 🐶,for your continued support of my musical art which comes in many forms.

Dr. Malia Jade Roberson is a music theorist and founder of Music Theory Shop. She's a Lecturer in Performing Arts, Music, at *California State University, Channel Islands,* and teaches music theory, aural skills, and piano. Questions, comments, or to get music theory support, visit www.musictheoryshop.com.

Welcome, musicians.

You have this book because music is important to you. For some of you, music is not just your passion, it is your life. You can't possibly imagine yourself doing anything else. You care deeply about this art form and as a serious musician, have dedicated your life to the study of music.

No matter where we are at in our musical journeys, there is always something to learn. *Musicians are lifelong learners.*

There are many roles for musicians; we're performers, composers, singer-songwriters, poets, music producers, educators, scholars, philosophers...we're artists. Our art is a reflection of the life surrounding us, and our contribution to the fabric of our culture cannot be understated and it should never be undervalued. No matter what kind of musical art we create, it is our artistic responsibility to gather, study, and hone as many musical skills as possible in order to produce our best work. The world requires our art. In fact, *the world needs our art now more than ever.*

Musicians are lifelong learners.

I wrote this book focusing on the most foundational material in Western music: scales and modes, because mastering these materials is the beginning to unlocking true freedom in music-making. If you want to feel less stress and ease in performance, composition, improvisation, instrumental technique, and aural skills (ear training), then you must take some time to develop your "**musical fluency**" which starts with the materials of music. Strong musical fluency gives you the ability to "speak music" in the moment, that is, instinctually, reactively, rather than laboriously. Anybody can do this. It only takes time and intentional practice to develop musical fluency.

Practice the foundational materials in this book until you no longer need to reference the book. Imagine the ability to sit down and read any piece of music you want (sight reading). Imagine writing music from what you hear in your head, to putting it down on paper without relying on technology or an instrument (aural skills). Imagine learning music in a fraction of the time it takes you now (strategic music learning). Imagine the ability to communicate with other musicians and describe musical ideas for collaboration (theory). Imagine the ability to figure out how any piece of music works (music analysis). This is all possible when the foundational materials are locked into your longterm memory so that they are instantly accessible and applied in the split second moments of music-making.

Feel a sense of freedom in music-making.

I used to think that my piano teacher only gave me scales to practice to develop finger dexterity. While that's partly true, I now understand that scales are foundational to the Western major-minor tonal system. If this foundation isn't solid, it makes continued study more difficult since the study of music is cumulative. The good news is, you can always return to these foundational materials and continue to see significant results in your musicianship. You do not need to know how to read music to get through this book from cover to cover. See the graphics and letters and go for it. I want you to absorb this material by getting it into your body through instrumental and vocal performance. *The reading and writing will follow.* If you already read, your skills will strengthen. The ultimate goal of this approach, by studying 9 scales and modes from a single tonic, is to fully experience the idea, sound, and feeling of "being in a key" in a kind of "musical meditation" through intentional practice, one tonic at a time. In so doing, this deep dive into all 30 major and minor keys will help you master the *Circle of 5ths* and the relationships between keys to better understand more advanced techniques, like modulation.

"Musically meditate" on one key at a time.

When you can get a handle on scales, *chord construction* becomes easier. Get a handle on chord construction, and *chord progressions* (functional harmony - harmonic syntax) become easier. Get a handle on chord progressions and the full spectrum of *functional harmony* becomes your artistic palette. Your creativity is only limited by your own imagination.

The 9 Western scales and modes presented in this book are just the tip of the iceberg when it comes to organized pitch. There are endless possibilities for constructing scales and modes both Western and non-Western that are beyond the scope of this book. It is my hope that this book will inspire you to experiment through improvisation; try modifying the scales and modes presented here. I also hope that the book will spark your curiosity to seek more knowledge about non-Western pitch collections, tuning systems, instruments, and genres of music.

So let's get comfortable with all 30 major-minor keys and have fun at the same time. Be sure to keep close track of your progress using the two practice charts in this book. Below is a 5-step strategy of holistic practice to reinforce the connection of theory (mental, internal) to practice (action, realization). As you work through this book, the end-goal is to perform all of the following tasks with "flow" (no hesitations, no mechanical resistance, and committed to memory) for each tonic. Are you ready? Let's go!

*(1) **Play** through the same-tonic scales and modes on your instrument individually, and as one exercise set. Use ascending and descending motion at least one octave.*
*(2) **Improvise** on each scale and mode. In the moment, play melodic fragments from each scale and mode. Have fun and don't overthink it.*
*(3) **Sing** **a capella** (without an instrument) through all of the same-tonic scales and modes on the given solfege, scale degree numbers, or letter names (singing will improve your ear).*
(4) Using a key signature, write out each scale and mode in music notation by hand.
*(5) For all previous tasks, be able to **identify** any scale degree in any key. For example, what is "mi" in E major? Be able to play, write, sing, and identify by ear.*

Get "off book" as soon as you can and start using your favorite scales and modes in your music!

Here is my best advice, practical strategies, and inner mindset work that will help you not only finish this book, but cultivate your work ethic and study approach for the future, wherever music takes you:

Find JOY in the process of learning.

- **Review** often. If some piece of information is truly too opaque for you to understand no matter how much you study, it just means that you're not ready for the information. Go back and review. Build confidence on previous material and return later. Do not think of this as moving backwards, it does not mean regression. Rather, this is called reinforcement. Re-strengthening the foundational layers is sometimes required before significant progress can be made.

- Give yourself **grace** for periods of inconsistency. We know that consistency (related to organization, planning, and keeping promises to yourself) is the only way to make progress and experience deep musical growth. But we are human beings. It is quite common for artists to experience periods of both inspired work that feels like effortless creativity, like, "wow, I just wrote a song in 20 minutes," to inactive periods, like, "ugh, I haven't touched my instrument in 2 weeks." This is the up and down cycle of an artist, like life itself. It's important to realize that the inactive periods are necessary for inner growth. Inactivity may allow for new ideas to blossom, to "marinate" on existing ideas, to plan with intention and strategy, and to clear space (in all senses) for the new. Welcome those "non-productive" periods and give yourself grace to regroup. It never means regression. As you know, there are so many different musical skills to develop that it is best when they are in rotation to avoid burnout.

- Have **patience** for a payoff that is likely years (or even decades) down the road. The lack of patience is the main reason students don't want to practice music (theory, instrument, aural skills). It's not boredom. It's the lack of patience to be able to sit with the uncomfortable parts of music study, like playing scales. Why spend time doing something that isn't going to result in learning a song? Understand that we're not focused on learning one song; *we are working on the skills that will help you learn 10,000 songs.*

- Find **joy** in the process of learning (that is the secret sauce to "patience"). Record yourself (video or audio) at the start of studying this book, record throughout, and record after you complete the book. Appreciate all of the seemingly small steps of improvement you achieved along the way. They really add up to make a huge difference in your overall musicianship. Never stop learning.

Good luck, musicians!

malia

Review Grace
Patience
Joy

Hello, music educators!

This method book is an excellent supplement for music lessons (all instruments & voice), group piano & keyboard proficiency, music theory, music education, and aural skills classes. It was especially designed **for students transitioning from Music Fundamentals to Theory I**, *with the intention to gain a deeper fluency in all 30 major and minor keys.* I've made several decisions about this approach that will help you decide if this book will work to meet your student outcomes.

- 9 heptatonic scales and modes, Western diatonic 7 modes + harmonic & melodic minor.
- Moveable "do" solfege, "do-based" minor.
- Piano prioritized, piano keyboard layouts and color for visual learners. Piano fingerings are not included in order to accommodate all instruments and to avoid confusion with scale degrees.
- Study of all diatonic and chromatic pitches from one tonic.
- 6 concise theory lessons (fundamentals) focusing on the melodic dimension of music.
- Western modes as derivatives of the major and natural minor scales (all from one tonic).
- Western modes in the context of the 15 major keys.
- Theoretical keys replaced by enharmonic equivalents.
- Some theoretical modes included if their major/minor scale from the same tonic exists.
- Conversational prose, interleaved pedagogy, equitable learning for multiple learning styles.
- One semester completion with strategized practice - intermediate & advanced students.
- Two practice charts are included to mark progress. These help with both structured and self-paced work.

For music theory courses:

Use actively (students can perform, write, improvise) as a supplement for Music Fundamentals at the introduction of key signatures, AP Music Theory, overlapping into the first course in a theory sequence after Fundamentals, and intro jazz theory course. This can be a helpful reference tool for advanced theory courses.

For keyboard proficiency, piano lessons, voice/instrumental lessons, and aural skills:

Intermediate and advanced students can usually get through one tonic per week, performing one octave ascending and descending. I would suggest this as a two-semester supplement for group piano proficiency courses of music majors or students that have some musical experience (not complete beginners). There are 18 tonics, but I suggest doubling up on enharmonic equivalents to reduce the workload. For deeper study, include melodic improvisation exercises and listen + play (play or sing a melodic fragment from one scale or mode and have students copy). For group piano, have students play all of the scales and modes from one tonic in sync. Create "challenges" for students to demonstrate their skills and play with varying tempo, rhythm, and dynamics. Since singing is easily transposed, students should be able to sing all 9 scale and mode types within a few weeks. Supplement solfege with written notation exercises that emphasize proper spelling and key signatures. Other tasks could include: accompanying themselves on piano while singing, singing particular scales or modes to prepare for sight singing, and reinforcing intervallic relationships between scale degrees.

Questions, comments, or feedback?
Email Malia: musictheoryshop@gmail.com.

For kids and beginners 😄:

Skip the theory lessons for now. Use practice charts to gamify performance of scales and modes!

Table of Contents

Good luck, musicians!

Lesson 1: Music's magical number "7"

This lesson focuses on how to spell scales and modes using the 7-letter musical alphabet, and then mapping onto the piano keyboard (hereafter, "keyboard").

The process of spelling, or naming pitches in any scale or mode, is the same: use alphabetical order. The entire **musical alphabet** contains the first 7 letters of the alphabet: **A, B, C, D, E, F, G**, after which the alphabet repeats itself. This makes the musical alphabet cyclical. It repeats itself seven times resulting in a range of pitches that align with the range of the modern piano and the Western modern orchestra, from the lowest pitch on the contrabassoon, to the highest pitch of the piccolo.

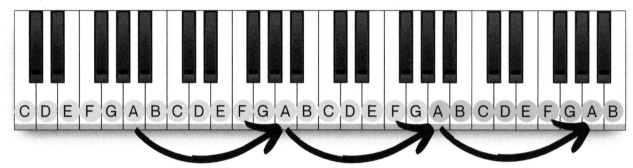

In the illustration above, the 7-letter musical alphabet is mapped onto the white keys of the keyboard. Keyboardists use the sets of 2 and 3 black keys as visual markers to map all "A's," all "B's," all "C's," and so forth, as they navigate the instrument. Note that the dots change color at each "A" key. The change in color illustrates the cyclical nature of the musical alphabet. The arrows further illustrate this cycle using "A" as a starting point and the next "A" as an ending point. This range is called an **octave**. Octave spans are not limited to "A;" they can begin anywhere and end at the beginning of the next cycle.

The 162 scales and modes presented in this book each use all 7 letters in alphabetical order, beginning on any letter. Please note that not all scales and modes are made up of 7 unique pitches; for example, pentatonic scales/modes use 5 unique pitches. The octatonic (AKA "diminished"), chromatic, and whole tone scales use a different number of pitches than 7. In this book, we'll only focus on 9 selected **heptatonic**, or 7-note, scales and modes. To help with spelling and musical notation, remember that there are only *7 possible letter configurations*:

A-B-C-D-E-F-**G**-A
B-C-D-E-F-**G**-A-B
C-D-E-F-**G**-A-B-C
D-E-**F**-**G**-A-B-C-D
E-F-**G**-A-B-C-D-E
F-**G**-A-B-C-D-E-F
G-A-B-C-D-E-F-**G**

Every scale and mode uses one of the seven letter orders presented here on the left. *"Wait, but aren't there 162 scales/modes in this book?"* Yes! We achieve 162 unique scales and modes through differing accidentals (sharps and flats, discussed below) which alter the notes to create so many unique possibilities and sounds. But it's good to know that you can first check your spelling and notation of scales and modes by making sure the letters are in proper order.

The starting point of a scale or mode is called a **tonic** (also known as scale degree 1). The 7-letter musical alphabet also means that there are 7 possible **sharps** (a ♯ raises a pitch by 1 half step), and 7 possible **flats** (a ♭ lowers a pitch by 1 half step). Playing scales and modes, in order, is a great first step in your technical exercises; but ultimately, work toward varying the order, melodic patterns, and rhythm in your practice.

Lesson 2: How tetrachords connect 9 scales & modes

This lesson focuses on connecting all 9 scales and modes using 5 possible tetrachords.

First, let's talk "steps": *whole steps* and *half steps*. On the right, each pair of dots is placed at a distance of one **half step**, also known as a "**semitone**." Half steps are easily visualized on the keyboard because they are always adjacent - they "touch" the next piano key. Half steps can ascend or descend.

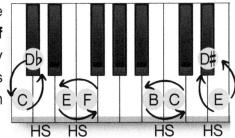

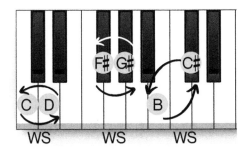

Stepwise motion – WS & HS

Here on the left, each pair of dots is placed at a distance of one **whole step**, also known as a "**whole tone**." A whole step is equal to 2 half steps. There is always one piano key in the middle. Although whole steps *skip* one piano key, they are still considered "steps."

Spelling is always important. Whole or half steps are "**diatonic**" when they belong to a specific key, using 7 different notes in alphabetical order. If the step has repeated letters (such as C to C♯), then that half step is "**chromatic**" (chromatic pitches are not in the "family" of 7 pitches that make a key). All diatonic steps are a distance, called an "**interval**," of 2 (second). A diatonic half step is called a **minor 2nd** (m2, "minor second"), and a diatonic whole step is called a **major 2nd** ("M2" for short). But before we dive into how to combine whole and half steps to create the 9 scale and mode types used in this book, let's simplify further by examining only *half* of a scale or mode, called a "**tetrachord.**"

A	B	C	D	E
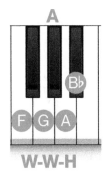	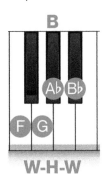	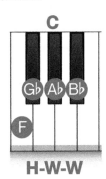		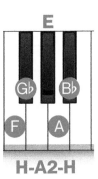
W-W-H	**W-H-W**	**H-W-W**	**W-W-W**	**H-A2-H**

A **tetrachord** is a 4-note scale (stepwise-motion "fragment" or "half of a scale."). It takes two of these tetrachords to create the 9 scale and mode types used in this book. In the Western major-minor tonal system of scales and modes, there are 5 main tetrachord types (presented in no hierarchical order): **(A) W-W-H; (B) W-H-W, (C) H-W-W; (D) W-W-W; (E) H-A2-H**. The "A" from "A2" in the last tetrachord (E) stands for "**augmented**" which increases a diatonic whole step an additional half step (A2=3 HS), but doesn't change the number. Note that there are two piano keys between G♭ and A.

How this works: Each scale/mode is a combination of two of the tetrachords above, separated by one whole step (except Lydian & Locrian which are separated by one half step). Notice the commonalities: for example, major and melodic minor both end with "A;" the "B" tetrachord is the most widely used; Locrian and Lydian are surprisingly similar, both use "D."

MAJOR SCALE	**A + A**
MIXOLYDIAN MODE	**A + B**
LYDIAN MODE	**D + A**
MELODIC MINOR SCALE	**B + A**
HARMONIC MINOR	**B + E**
SCALE DORIAN MODE	**B + B**
NATURAL MINOR SCALE	**B + C**
PHRYGIAN MODE	**C + C**
LOCRIAN MODE	**C + D**

2

MAJOR SCALE	A + A
MIXOLYDIAN MODE	A + B
LYDIAN MODE	D + A
MELODIC MINOR SCALE	B + A
HARMONIC MINOR SCALE	B + E
DORIAN MODE	B + B
NATURAL MINOR SCALE	B + C
PHRYGIAN MODE	C + C
LOCRIAN MODE	C + D

Using a "D" tonic, study the tetrachords that, when combined, make up 9 scale and modes.

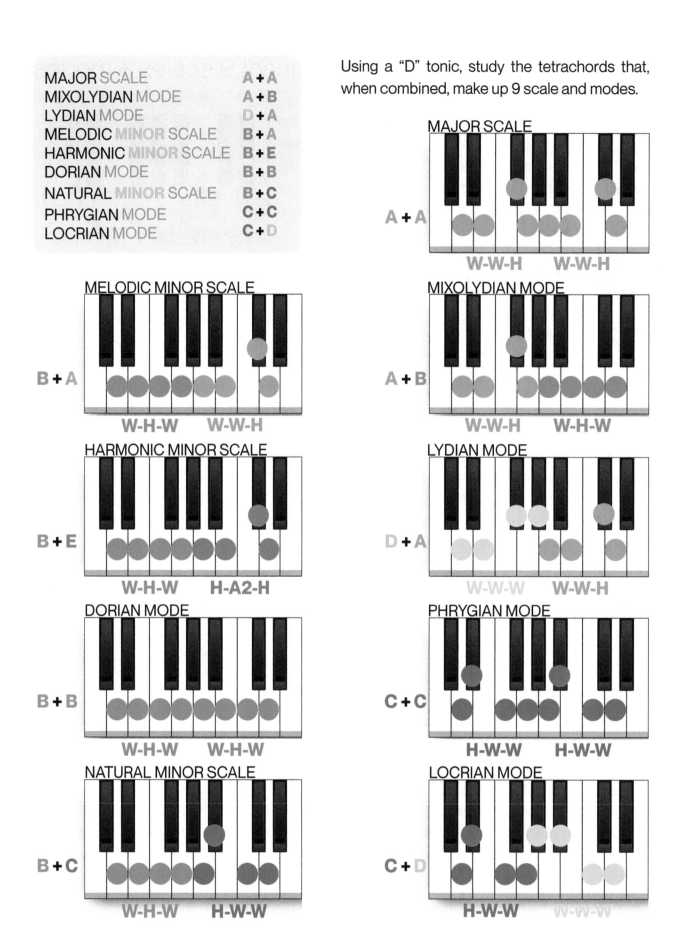

MAJOR SCALE

A + A

W-W-H W-W-H

MELODIC MINOR SCALE

B + A

W-H-W W-W-H

MIXOLYDIAN MODE

A + B

W-W-H W-H-W

HARMONIC MINOR SCALE

B + E

W-H-W H-A2-H

LYDIAN MODE

D + A

W-W-W W-W-H

DORIAN MODE

B + B

W-H-W W-H-W

PHRYGIAN MODE

C + C

H-W-W H-W-W

NATURAL MINOR SCALE

B + C

W-H-W H-W-W

LOCRIAN MODE

C + D

H-W-W W-W-W

It's not important to memorize the "X+Y" tetrachord formulas; rather, notice the commonalities between them. Mentally map the whole and half step distances onto the keyboard which will help later with notation on the musical staff. Play on your instrument! Improvise with these 5 tetrachord types and then combine in pairs (and this is just the beginning!). Can you imagine playing the same whole and half step configurations from different tonics?

Lesson 5: Two ways to construct modes

This lesson illustrates how modes can be constructed as derivatives of the major and natural minor scales, the "single tonic approach," and compares this approach alongside modes contructed in the context of a key.

The "*single tonic approach*" used in this book explores 9 types of scale-step formulas all from one starting point. Studying and practicing this way allows the student to perform the most common melodic configurations in Western music by deepening the understanding of diatonic versus chromatic pitches, and most importantly, the idea and sensation of "being in a key." You can imagine this type of practicing as a "tonic meditation" -- a focused study on the complete chromatic set with the diatonic subsets it contains. This activity emphasizes and privileges the major-minor tonal system (modes 1 & 6) that dominates Western music. While it is equally important to study and practice modes in the context of how they function in a key, (presented in the last part of this book), the practice method in the single tonic approach works more as a way to reinforce the major and minor pitch collections.

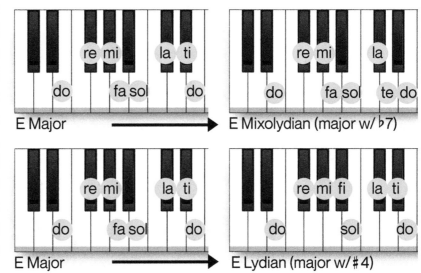

E Major ⟶ E Mixolydian (major w/ ♭7)

E Major ⟶ E Lydian (major w/ ♯4)

In the single tonic approach, modes beginning with **W-W-H**, the same tetrachord as the major scale (like mixolydian), or a M3 "do" & "mi" (like lydian), will be constructed as "major with chromatic alterations." For example, we can think of the mixolydian mode as a derivative of the major scale with a chromatic alteration of scale degree ♭7, "te." Modes beginning with **W-H-W**, the natural minor tetrachord (like dorian), or that have the m3 ("do" to "me" between scale degrees 1 and 3), (like phrygian & locrian), will be built as natural minor with chromatic alterations.

Major Mixolydian Lydian

E Natural Minor ⟶ E Dorian (minor w/♯ 6 "la")

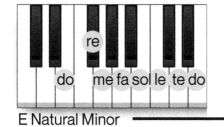

E Natural Minor ⟶ E Phrygian (minor w/♭ 2 "ra")

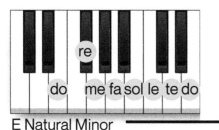

E Natural Minor ⟶ E Locrian (minor w/♭ 2 &♭ 5 "ra" & "se")

Minor Dorian Phrygian Locrian

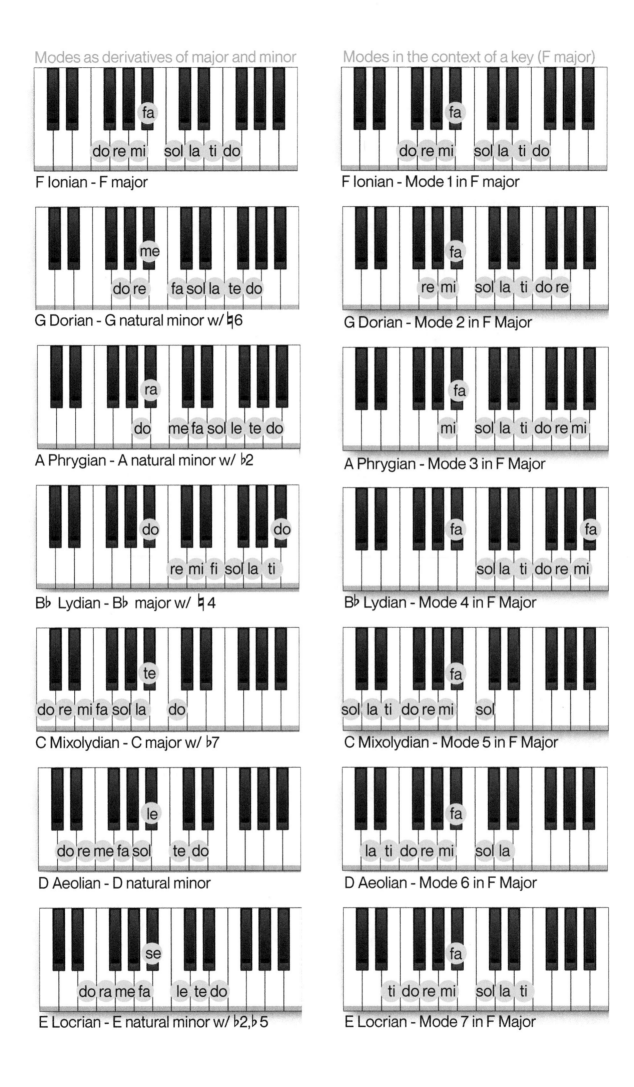

Lesson 6: Owning the Circle of 5ths

This lesson discusses the idea of "key," the organization and use of the Circle of 5ths, and maps the pattern of 5ths onto the keyboard.

The **Circle of 5ths** is a clock-like graphic of all 30 major and minor keys. It is the cornerstone of Western music theory fundamentals and the gateway to advanced musical study of the major-minor tonal system. But let me start by saying that the Circle of 5ths chart is just a memory aid. Your end goal is to one day *never* have to reference this chart again because the information is locked into your long-term memory through practice and musical experience. You will instantly be able to access this basic information and immediately apply it to music creation, improvisation, performance, and dialoging with other musicians. *Anybody* with the desire can do this.

15 Major & 15 Minor Keys

The Circle of 5ths is exciting because it quite quickly allows you to see pervasive patterns in music. The musical alphabet of 7 letters replicates itself over and over around the Circle. The clock-like image implies the idea of motion, of moving in time, which we'll explore soon. There are two ways to understand and apply the Circle: (1) as a chart that illustrates the relationships between keys, each letter representing a "key" consisting of 7 members (pitches); (2) as a chart that illustrates harmonic motion (chord progressions), each letter representing the **root** of a chord. First, let's study how the Circle illustrates the relationship between keys.

A **key** is a diatonic collection of 7 unique members (pitches), each member having a special role (think of each member as having its own personality and characteristics). Each key is named by its tonic. Each upper case letter on the perimeter represents a major key, with a total of 15 major keys. Each lower case letter inside the perimeter of the Circle represents a minor key, and with a corresponding total of 15 minor keys.

The numbers on the interior of the Circle represent the number of sharps ♯ or flats ♭ in each **key signature**. The key signature is a notational shortcut that lists all of the sharps or flats in a key, presented at the beginning of each musical staff, in an effort to streamline the music reading and writing process. In this version of the Circle, the black letters are "sharp keys" (having sharps ♯ in their key signatures) and the fuchsia letters are "flat keys" (having flats ♭ in their key signatures.)

Key Relationships

Notice that the upper and lower case letters are grouped in pairs: C/a, F/d.

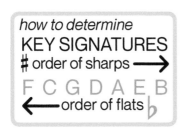

how to determine
KEY SIGNATURES
♯ order of sharps ⟶
F C G D A E B
⟵ order of flats ♭

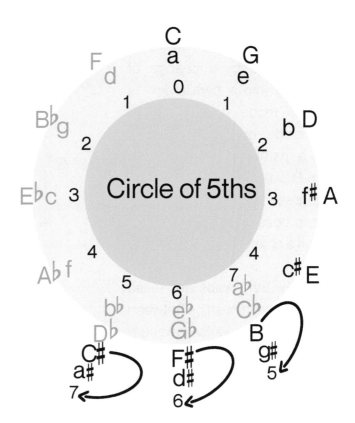

Circle of 5ths

G/e, etc. This special grouping illustrates an important relationship between these two keys: grouped keys on the Circle are called "relative keys" because they share the same key signature. The minor relative key is actually Mode 6 (aeolian) of the relative major. Relative keys are the most often go-to choice for **modulation**, a process of changing keys, usually in a new phrase or entire section. A temporary change of key, usually within the same phrase but not confirmed with a **cadence** (closure), is called **tonicization**.

The ability to change keys adds dimension and variety in music by playing with the listener's expectations. Changing to a relative key is a subtle way to create variety because all of the pitches are the same; the listener simply reorients the ear to a new tonic. There are other possibilities for creating a subtle modulation to any **closely related** key.

Any adjacent key on the Circle (any key to the left or right) is considered closely related: they have 6 of the same pitches. This means that every key has 5 closely related keys (e.g. D's closely related keys: b, G, e, A, f#). Modulation to a closely related key is the least obtrusive both for performers and listeners because of their shared pitch content ("common tones"). This provides a sensation of equal balance between "change" and "familiarity."

For a more surprising effect, modulation to a **distantly related** key can create instant drama. Distantly related keys are further apart on the Circle, and in fact, keys that are "opposite" are the *most* distantly related (tonics are a **tritone** apart=3 WS). The most commonly practiced distantly related key change is the use of **parallel keys**. Parallel keys are one major and one minor key that share the same tonic (e.g., G to g). A change to the parallel key is not considered modulation, however, which is defined by a change of tonic. Shifting into a parallel key is a change of mode, from the major to minor mode, or vice versa. This shift into a parallel key can be quite stunning. However, if the tonic triad (scale degrees 1-3-5) remains intact, then the process is modal mixture, rather than a change of key.

The Circle of 5ths maps out these very important relationships between keys and presents a logical arrange-

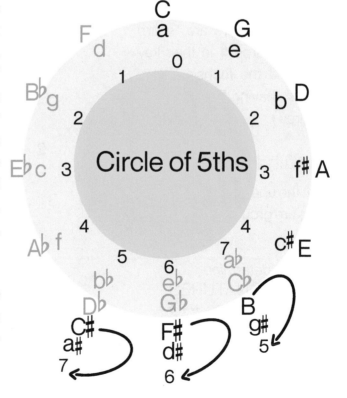

Key relationships in the Circle of 5ths, tonics moving in P5s (perfect 5ths)

(keyboard diagram with notes: C → G → D → A → E → B, then Cb, Gb/F#)

● = sharp♯ keys   ● = flat♭ keys

(second keyboard diagram with notes: Db/C#, Ab/G#, Eb/D#, Bb/A#, F)

The Circle of 5ths "uncoiled" and layed out on the keyboard. G♯, D♯, & A♯ do not exist as major key tonics; however, they do serve as minor key tonics. F is an enharmonic equivalent to E♯, and at that point, the P5's "U-turn" to account for the remaining flat keys.

ment of increasing the number of accidentals as the keys progress around the circle. The organization of tonics in this book is ordered by the Circle of 5ths beginning with C, and working down the right with "sharp keys," followed by working down the left with "flat keys."

Harmonic Motion

V–I examples: G to C; C to F; D to G

The second way to understand and use the Circle of 5ths is to construct **harmonic progressions** (chord progressions). Harmonic progressions are a sequence of chords that create a sense of momentum, of "goal-oriented" motion, implied in the term "progression." Harmonic progressions raise musical expectations that when met, feel satisfying with a strong sense of closure. When these expectations are not met, the sensation can feel surprising and create yet more anticipation for another attempt at closure.

Root motion by 5th (P5) in the V-I dominant to tonic motion is the most conclusive goal-oriented motion in Western music and creates the strongest sense of closure. Emulating the V-I progression with other chords from the Circle of 5ths is quite easy. Consider any letter as the root of a major triad. Every dominant V is the letter to the right, so to create a V-I progression, play any major triad and move counterclockwise (left) to resolve it. Continue the pattern of 5ths. Note that the "uncoiled" keyboard mapping above illustrates relationships of keys and the arrows progress opposite of goal-oriented harmonic motion.

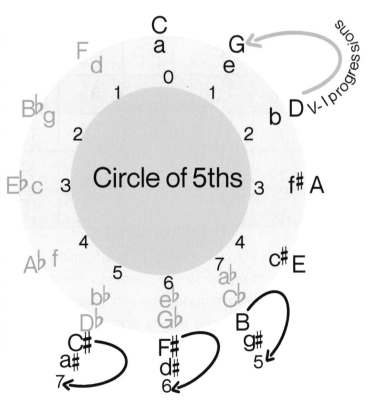

Use this chart to strategize
your practice for the
most efficient study.

tonic	major scale	mixolydian mode	lydian mode	melodic minor	harmonic minor	dorian mode	natural minor	phrygian mode	locrian mode
C	C	C	C	C	C	C	C	C	C
G	G	G	G	G	G	G	G	G	G
D	D	D	D	D	D	D	D	D	D
A	A	A	A	A	A	A	A	A	A
E	E	E	E	E	E	E	E	E	E
B	B	B	B	B	B	B	B	B	B
F#	F#	F#	F#	F#	F#	F#	F#	F#	F#
C#	C#	C#	C#	C#	C#	C#	C#	C#	C#
G#	Ab	Ab	Ab	G#	G#	G#	G#	G#	G#
D#	Eb	Eb	Eb	D#	D#	D#	D#	D#	D#
A#	Bb	Bb	Bb	A#	A#	A#	A#	A#	A#
F	F	F	F	F	F	F	F	F	F
Bb	Bb	Bb	Bb	Bb	Bb	Bb	Bb	Bb	Bb
Eb	Eb	Eb	Eb	Eb	Eb	Eb	Eb	Eb	Eb
Ab	Ab	Ab	Ab	Ab	Ab	Ab	Ab	Ab	Ab
Db	Db	Db	Db	C#	C#	C#	C#	C#	C#
Gb	Gb	Gb	Gb	F#	F#	F#	F#	F#	F
Cb	Cb	Cb	Cb	B	B	B	B	B	B

Begin working in rows, left to right, performing scales and modes from one tonic. Be sure to combine sets of enharmonic equivalents to reduce your workload: B/Cb; F#/Gb; C#/Db; G#/Ab; D#/Eb. Once you have mastered each "tonic," plan to play each scale or mode by type, moving top to bottom by column. Finally, plan to play all scales and modes in random order. Consider performing in a variety of ways on your instrument and singing. Perform in strict time using a metronome, in "swing time," and/or other rhythm.

My favorite SCALES

My favorite MODES

Relative Keys: C Major/A Minor
Parallel Keys: C Major/C Minor

C Scales & C Modes

C Major Scale
C-D-E-F-G-A-B-C

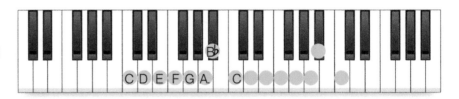

C Mixolydian Mode
C-D-E-F-G-A-B♭-C

C Lydian Mode
C-D-E-F♯-G-A-B-C

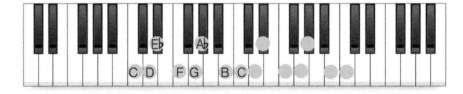

C Melodic Minor
C-D-E♭-F-G-A-B-C

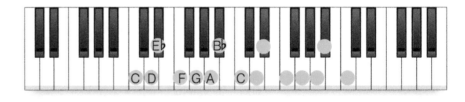

C Harmonic Minor
C-D-E♭-F-G-A♭-B-C

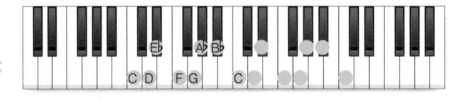

C Dorian Mode
C-D-E♭-F-G-A-B♭-C

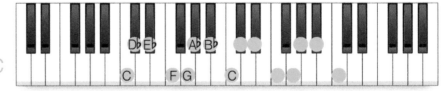

C Natural Minor
C-D-E♭-F-G-A♭-B♭-C

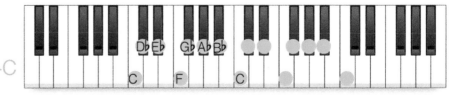

C Phrygian Mode
C-D♭-E♭-F-G-A♭-B♭-C

C Locrian Mode
C-D♭-E♭-F-G♭-A♭-B♭-C

C Scales & C Modes

G Scales & G Modes

G Major Scale
G-A-B-C-D-E-F♯-G

G Mixolydian Mode
G-A-B-C-D-E-F-G

G Lydian Mode
G-A-B-C♯-D-E-F♯-G

G Melodic Minor
G-A-B♭-C-D-E-F♯-G

G Harmonic Minor
G-A-B♭-C-D-E♭-F♯-G

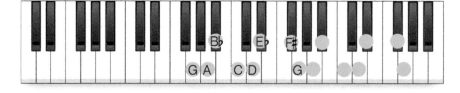

G Dorian Mode
G-A-B♭-C-D-E-F-G

G Natural Minor
G-A-B♭-C-D-E♭-F-G

G Phrygian Mode
G-A♭-B♭-C-D-E♭-F-G

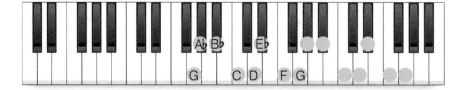

G Locrian Mode
G-A♭-B♭-C-D♭-E♭-F-G

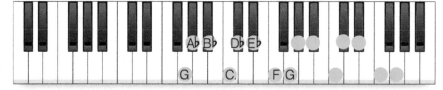

G Scales & G Modes

G Major

G Mixolydian
Major with ♮7

G Lydian
Major with #4

G Melodic Minor

G Harmonic Minor

G Dorian
Natural Minor with ♮6

G Natural Minor

G Phrygian
Natural Minor with ♭2

G Locrian
Natural Minor with ♭2 and ♭5

D Scales & D Modes

D Major Scale
D-E-F#-G-A-B-C#-D

D Mixolydian Mode
D-E-F#-G-A-B-C-D

D Lydian Mode
D-E-F#-G#-A-B-C#-D

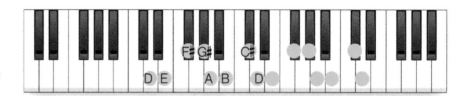

D Melodic Minor
D-E-F-G-A-B-C#-D

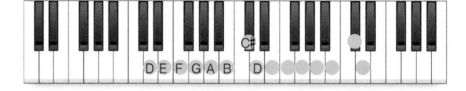

D Harmonic Minor
D-E-F-G-A-Bb-C#-D

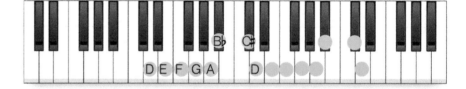

D Dorian Mode
D-E-F-G-A-B-C-D

D Natural Minor
D-E-F-G-A-Bb-C-D

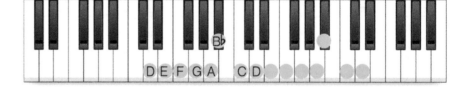

D Phrygian Mode
D-Eb-F-G-A-Bb-C-D

D Locrian Mode
D-Eb-F-G-Ab-Bb-C-D

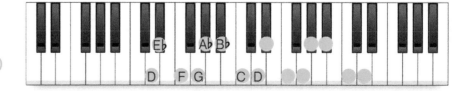

D Scales & D Modes

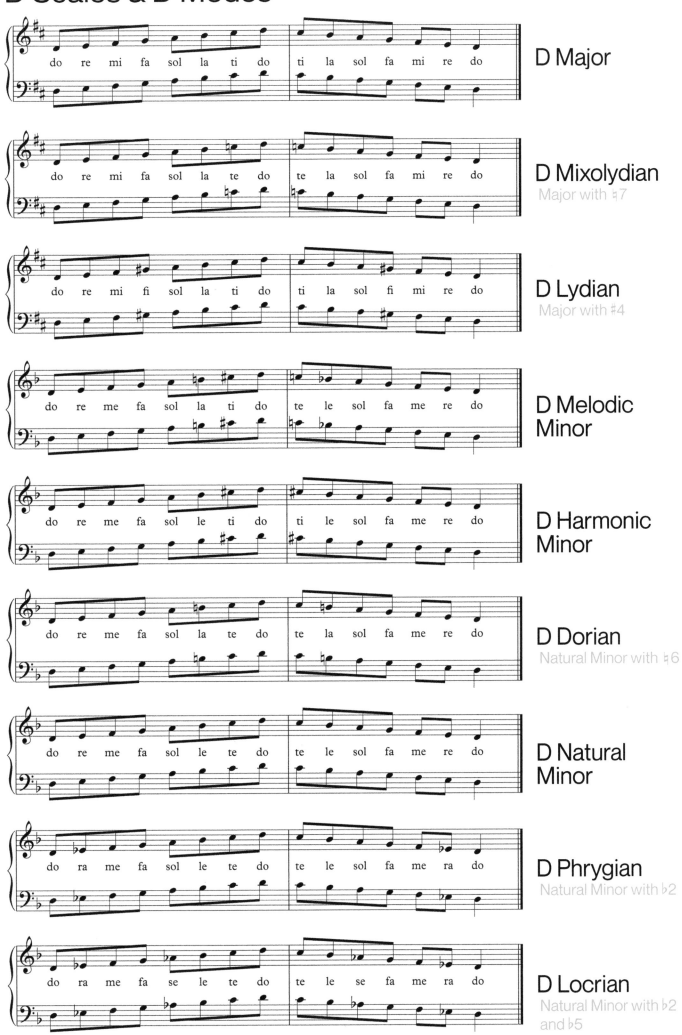

D Major

D Mixolydian
Major with ♭7

D Lydian
Major with #4

D Melodic
Minor

D Harmonic
Minor

D Dorian
Natural Minor with ♮6

D Natural
Minor

D Phrygian
Natural Minor with ♭2

D Locrian
Natural Minor with ♭2
and ♭5

Relative Keys: A Major/F♯ Minor
Parallel Keys: A Major/A Minor

A Scales & A Modes

A Major Scale
A-B-C♯-D-E-F♯-G♯-A

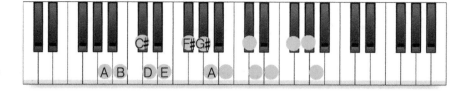

A Mixolydian Mode
A-B-C♯-D-E-F♯-G-A

A Lydian Mode
A-B-C♯-D♯-E-F♯-G♯-A

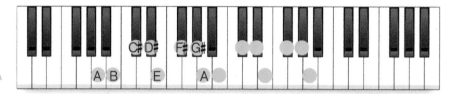

A Melodic Minor
A-B-C-D-E-F♯-G♯-A

A Harmonic Minor
A-B-C-D-E-F-G♯-A

A Dorian Mode
A-B-C-D-E-F♯-G-A

A Natural Minor
A-B-C-D-E-F-G-A

A Phrygian Mode
A-B♭-C-D-E-F-G-A

A Locrian Mode
A-B♭-C-D-E♭-F-G-A

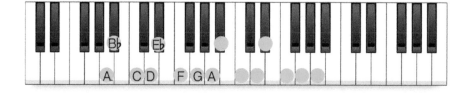

A Scales & A Modes

A Major

A Mixolydian
Major with ♮7

A Lydian
Major with #4

A Melodic Minor

A Harmonic Minor

A Dorian
Natural Minor with #6

A Natural Minor

A Phrygian
Natural Minor with ♭2

A Locrian
Natural Minor with ♭2 and ♭5

E Scales & E Modes

E Major Scale
E-F#-G#-A-B-C#-D#-E

E Mixolydian Mode
E-F#-G#-A-B-C#-D-E

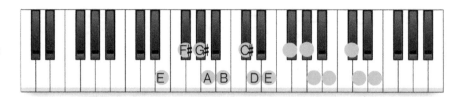

E Lydian Mode
E-F#-G#-A#-B-C#-D#-E

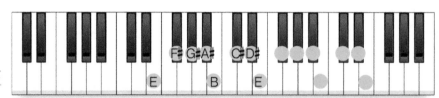

E Melodic Minor
E-F#-G-A-B-C#-D#-E

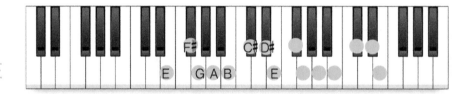

E Harmonic Minor
E-F#-G-A-B-C-D#-E

E Dorian Mode
E-F#-G-A-B-C#-D-E

E Natural Minor
E-F#-G-A-B-C-D-E

E Phrygian Mode
E-F-G-A-B-C-D-E

E Locrian Mode
E-F-G-A-Bb-C-D-E

E Scales & E Modes

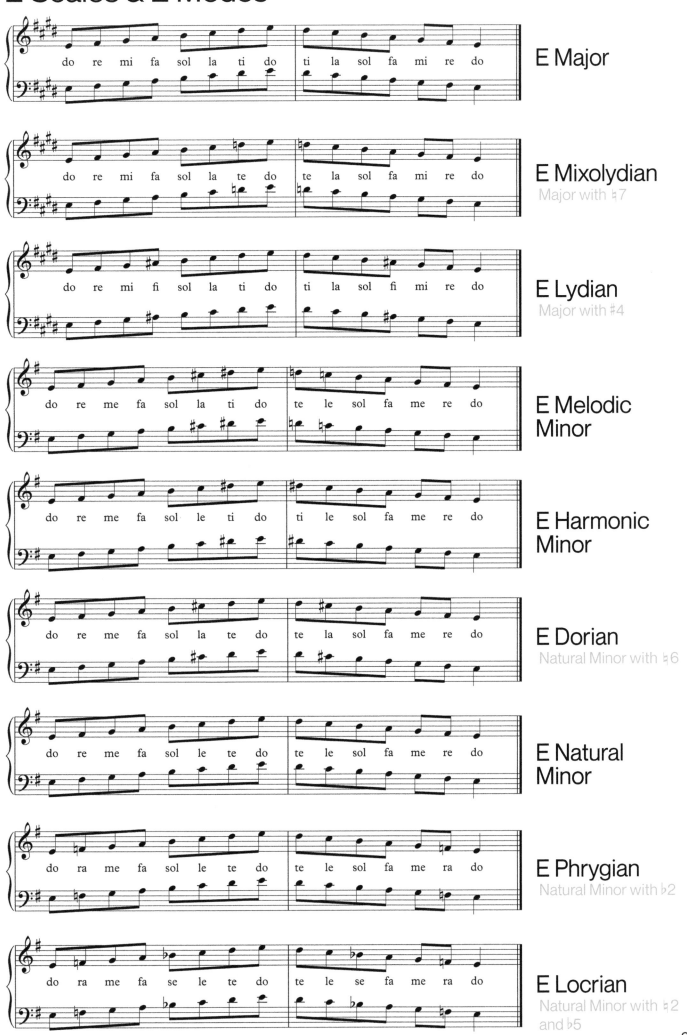

E Major

E Mixolydian
Major with ♭7

E Lydian
Major with #4

E Melodic
Minor

E Harmonic
Minor

E Dorian
Natural Minor with ♮6

E Natural
Minor

E Phrygian
Natural Minor with ♭2

E Locrian
Natural Minor with ♮2
and ♭5

B Scales & B Modes

B Major Scale
B-C#-D#-E-F#-G#-A#-B

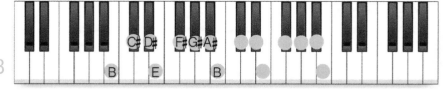

B Mixolydian Mode
B-C#-D#-E-F#-G#-A-B

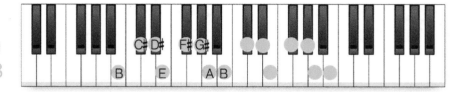

B Lydian Mode
B-C#-D#-E#-F#-G#-A#-B

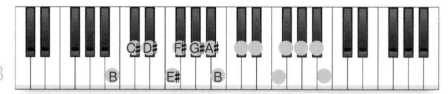

B Melodic Minor
B-C#-D-E-F#-G#-A#-B

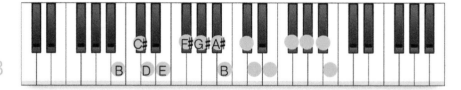

B Harmonic Minor
B-C#-D-E-F#-G-A#-B

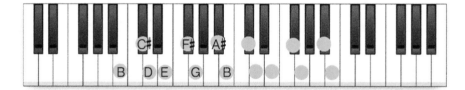

B Dorian Mode
B-C#-D-E-F#-G#-A-B

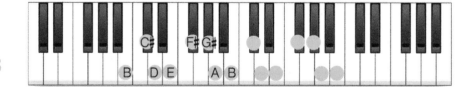

B Natural Minor
B-C#-D-E-F#-G-A-B

B Phrygian Mode
B-C-D-E-F#-G-A-B

B Locrian Mode
B-C-D-E-F-G-A-B

B Scales & B Modes

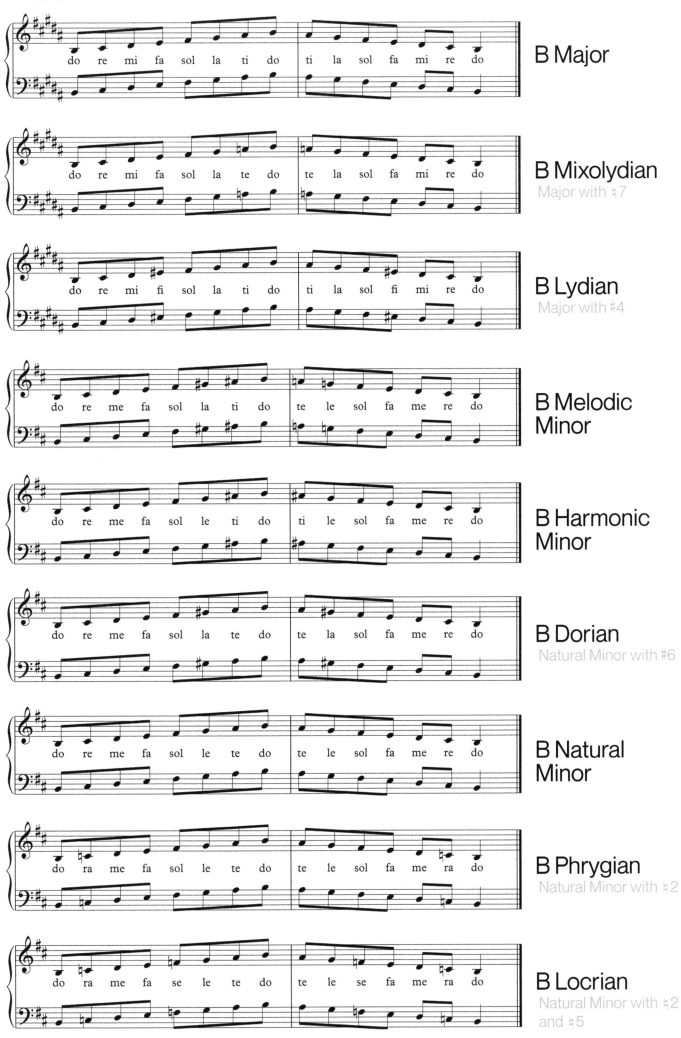

B Major

B Mixolydian
Major with ♮7

B Lydian
Major with #4

B Melodic
Minor

B Harmonic
Minor

B Dorian
Natural Minor with #6

B Natural
Minor

B Phrygian
Natural Minor with ♭2

B Locrian
Natural Minor with ♭2
and ♭5

24

F# Scales & F# Modes

F# Major Scale
F#-G#-A#-B-C#-D#-E#-F#

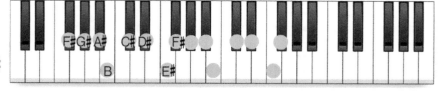

F# Mixolydian Mode
F#-G#-A#-B-C#-D#-E-F#

F# Lydian Mode
F#-G#-A#-B#-C#-D#-E#-F#

F# Melodic Minor
F#-G#-A-B-C#-D#-E#-F#

F# Harmonic Minor
F#-G#-A-B-C#-D-E#-F#

F# Dorian Mode
F#-G#-A-B-C#-D#-E-F#

F# Natural Minor
F#-G#-A-B-C#-D-E-F#

F# Phrygian Mode
F#-G-A-B-C#-D-E-F#

F# Locrian Mode
F#-G-A-B-C-D-E-F#

F# Scales & F# Modes

F# Major

F# Mixolydian
Major with ♭7

F# Lydian
Major with #4

F# Melodic Minor

F# Harmonic Minor

F# Dorian
Natural Minor with #6

F# Natural Minor

F# Phrygian
Natural Minor with ♭2

F# Locrian
Natural Minor with ♭2 and ♭5

26

Relative Keys: C# Major/A# Minor
Parallel Keys: C# Major/C# Minor

C# Scales & C# Modes

C# Major Scale
C#-D#-E#-F#-G#-A#-B#-C#

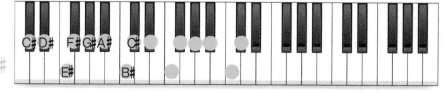

C# Mixolydian Mode
C#-D#-E#-F#-G#-A#-B-C#

C# Lydian Mode
C#-D#-E#-Fx-G#-A#-B#-C#

C# Melodic Minor
C#-D#-E-F#-G#-A#-B#-C#

C# Harmonic Minor
C#-D#-E-F#-G#-A-B#-C#

C# Dorian Mode
C#-D#-E-F#-G#-A#-B-C#

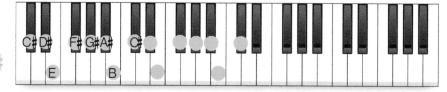

C# Natural Minor
C#-D#-E-F#-G#-A-B-C#

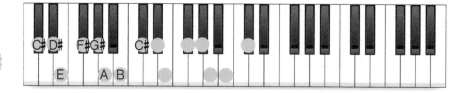

C# Phrygian Mode
C#-D-E-F#-G#-A-B-C#

C# Locrian Mode
C#-D-E-F#-G-A-B-C#

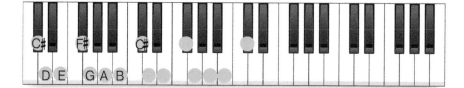

27

C# Scales & C# Modes

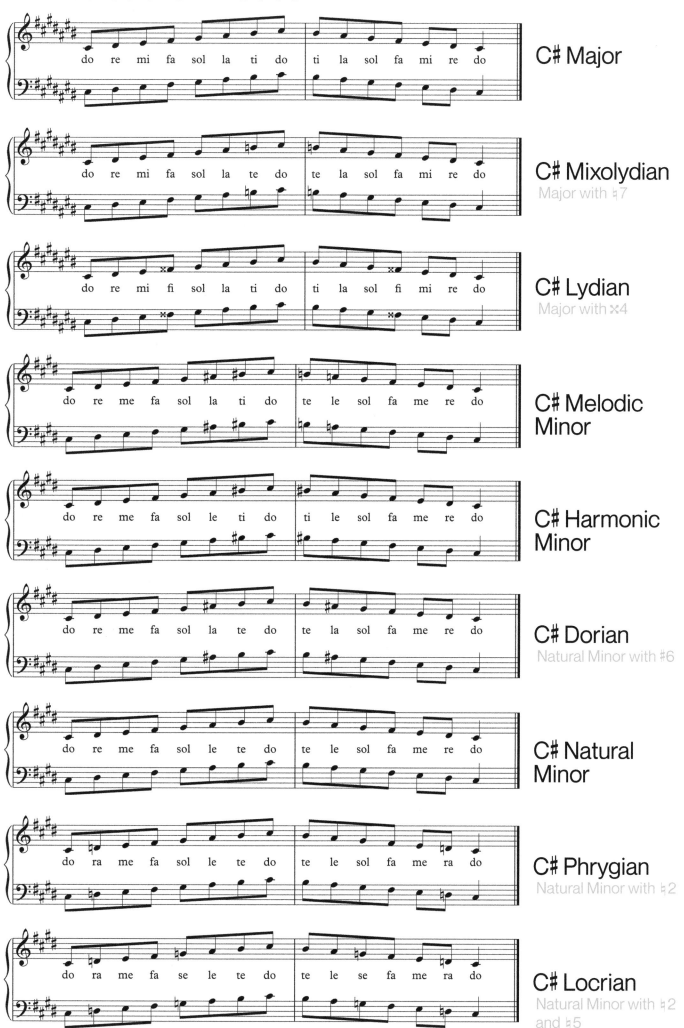

C# Major

C# Mixolydian
Major with ♭7

C# Lydian
Major with ×4

C# Melodic Minor

C# Harmonic Minor

C# Dorian
Natural Minor with #6

C# Natural Minor

C# Phrygian
Natural Minor with ♮2

C# Locrian
Natural Minor with ♮2 and ♮5

G# Scales & G# Modes

A♭ Major Scale
A♭-B♭-C-D♭-E♭-F-G-A♭

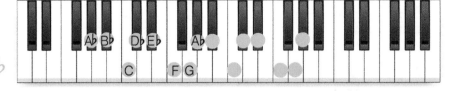

A♭ Mixolydian Mode
A♭-B♭-C-D♭-E♭-F-G-A♭

A♭ Lydian Mode
A♭-B♭-C-D-E♭-F-G-A♭

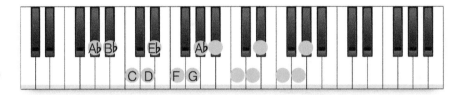

G# Melodic Minor
G#-A#-B-C#-D#-E#-Fx-G#

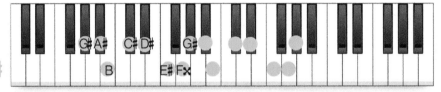

G# Harmonic Minor
G#-A#-B-C#-D#-E-Fx-G#

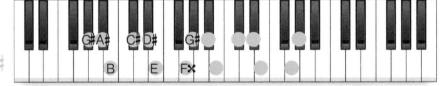

G# Dorian Mode
G#-A#-B-C#-D#-E#-F#-G#

G# Natural Minor
G#-A#-B-C#-D#-E-F#-G#

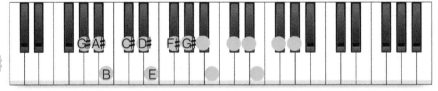

G# Phrygian Mode
G#-A-B-C#-D#-E-F#-G#

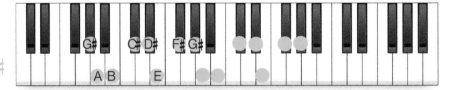

G# Locrian Mode
G#-A-B-C#-D-E-F#-G#

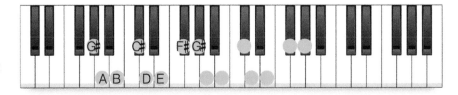

G♯ Scales & G♯ Modes

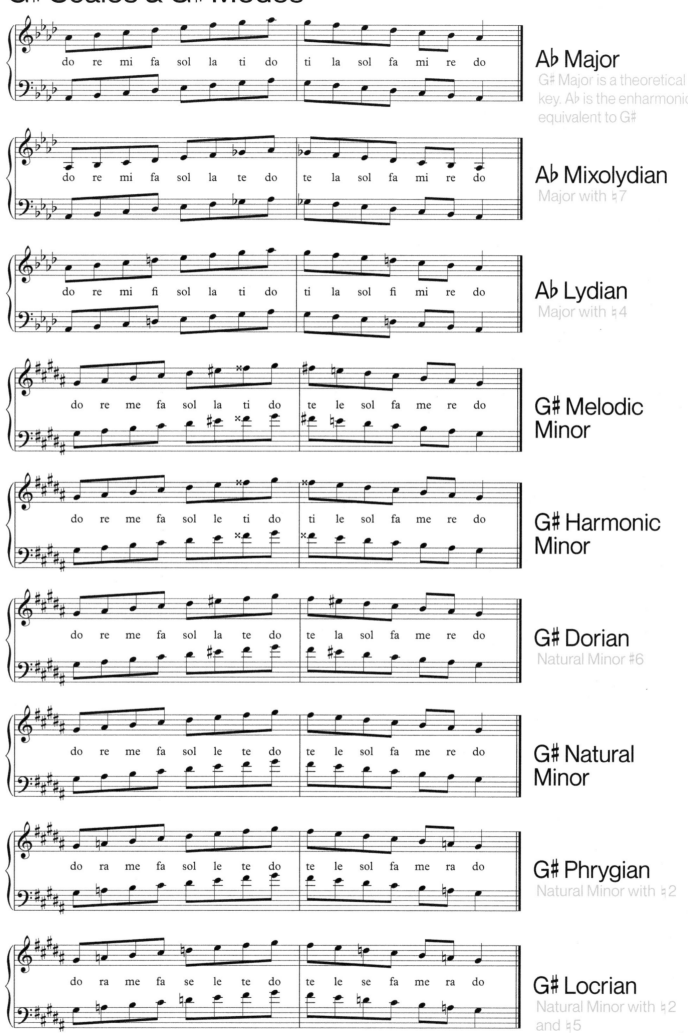

A♭ Major

A♭ Mixolydian
Major with ♭7

A♭ Lydian
Major with ♮4

G♯ Melodic Minor

G♯ Harmonic Minor

G♯ Dorian
Natural Minor #6

G♯ Natural Minor

G♯ Phrygian
Natural Minor with ♭2

G♯ Locrian
Natural Minor with ♭2 and ♭5

D♯ Scales & D♯ Modes

E♭ Major Scale
E♭-F-G-A♭-B♭-C-D-E♭

E♭ Mixolydian Mode
E♭-F-G-A♭-B♭-C-D♭-E♭

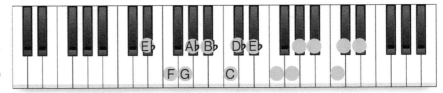

E♭ Lydian Mode
E♭-F-G-A-B♭-C-D-E♭

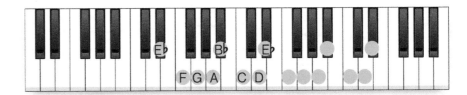

D♯ Melodic Minor
D♯-E♯-F♯-G♯-A♯-B♯-C𝄪-D♯

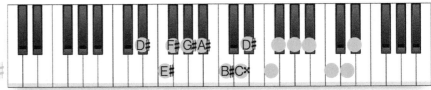

D♯ Harmonic Minor
D♯-E♯-F♯-G♯-A♯-B-C𝄪-D♯

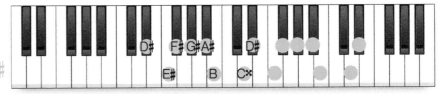

D♯ Dorian Mode
D♯-E♯-F♯-G♯-A♯-B♯-C♯-D♯

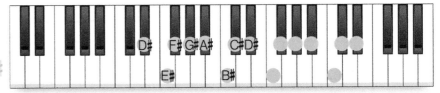

D♯ Natural Minor
D♯-E♯-F♯-G♯-A♯-B-C♯-D♯

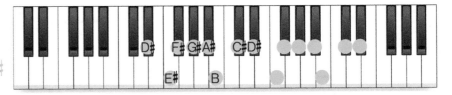

D♯ Phrygian Mode
D♯-E-F♯-G♯-A♯-B-C♯-D♯

D♯ Locrian Mode
D♯-E-F♯-G♯-A-B-C♯-D♯

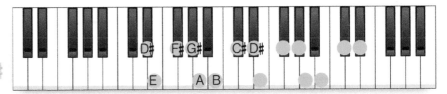

D# Scales & D# Modes

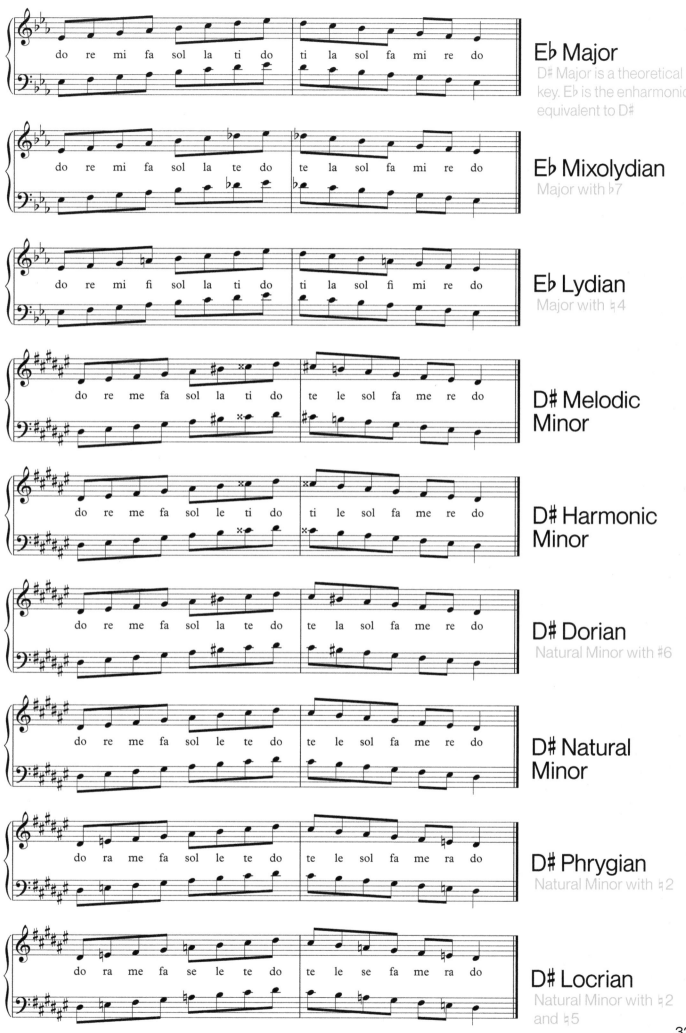

E♭ Major
D# Major is a theoretical key. E♭ is the enharmonic equivalent to D#

E♭ Mixolydian
Major with ♭7

E♭ Lydian
Major with ♮4

D# Melodic Minor

D# Harmonic Minor

D# Dorian
Natural Minor with #6

D# Natural Minor

D# Phrygian
Natural Minor with ♮2

D# Locrian
Natural Minor with ♮2 and ♮5

32

B♭ Major Scale
B♭-C-D-E♭-F-G-A-B♭

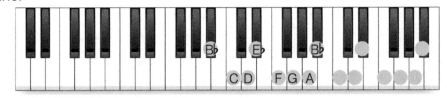

B♭ Mixolydian Mode
B♭-C-D-E♭-F-G-A♭-B♭

B♭ Lydian Mode
B♭-C-D-E-F-G-A-B♭

A♯ Melodic Minor
A♯-B♯-C♯-D♯-E♯-F𝄪-G𝄪-A♯

A♯ Harmonic Minor
A♯-B♯-C♯-D♯-E♯-F♯-G𝄪-A♯

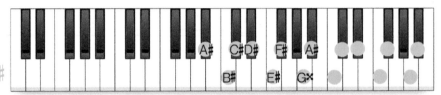

A♯ Dorian Mode
A♯-B♯-C♯-D♯-E♯-F𝄪-G♯-A♯

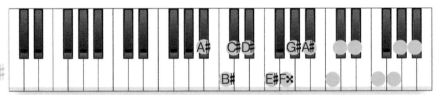

A♯ Natural Minor
A♯-B♯-C♯-D♯-E♯-F♯-G♯-A♯

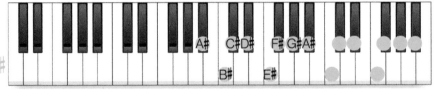

A♯ Phrygian Mode
A♯-B-C♯-D♯-E♯-F♯-G♯-A♯

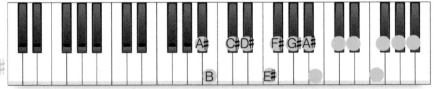

A♯ Locrian Mode
A♯-B-C♯-D♯-E-F♯-G♯-A♯

A♯ Scales & A♯ Modes

B♭ Major

A♯ Major is a theoretical key. B♭ is the enharmonic equivalent to A♯

do re mi fa sol la ti do | ti la sol fa mi re do

B♭ Mixolydian

Major with ♭7

do re mi fa sol la te do | te la sol fa mi re do

B♭ Lydian

Major with ♮4

do re mi fi sol la ti do | ti la sol fi mi re do

A♯ Melodic Minor

do re me fa sol la ti do | te le sol fa me re do

A♯ Harmonic Minor

do re me fa sol le ti do | ti le sol fa me re do

B♭ Dorian

Natural Minor with ♮6

do re me fa sol la te do | te la sol fa me re do

A♯ Natural Minor

do re me fa sol le te do | te le sol fa me re do

A♯ Phrygian

Natural Minor with ♮2

do ra me fa sol le te do | te le sol fa me ra do

A♯ Locrian

Natural Minor with ♮2 and ♮5

do ra me fa se le te do | te le se fa me ra do

34

F Scales & F Modes

Relative Keys: F Major/D Minor
Parallel Keys: F Major/F Minor

F Major Scale
F-G-A-B♭-C-D-E-F

F Mixolydian Mode
F-G-A-B♭-C-D-E♭-F

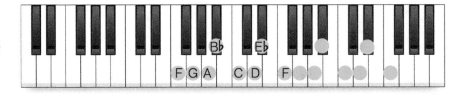

F Lydian Mode
F-G-A-B-C-D-E-F

F Melodic Minor
F-G-A♭-B♭-C-D-E-F

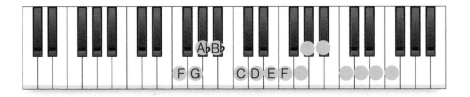

F Harmonic Minor
F-G-A♭-B♭-C-D♭-E-F

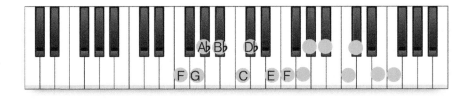

F Dorian Mode
F-G-A♭-B♭-C-D-E♭-F

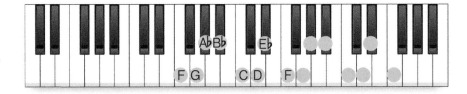

F Natural Minor
F-G-A♭-B♭-C-D♭-E♭-F

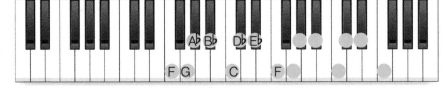

F Phrygian Mode
F-G♭-A♭-B♭-C-D♭-E♭-F

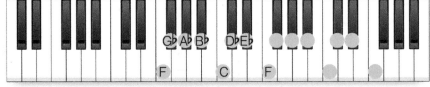

F Locrian Mode
F-G♭-A♭-B♭-C♭-D♭-E♭-F

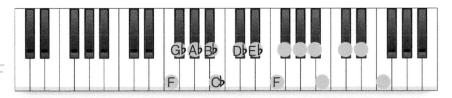

F Scales & F Modes

F Major

F Mixolydian
Major with ♭7

F Lydian
Major with ♮4

F Melodic Minor

F Harmonic Minor

F Dorian
Natural Minor with ♮6

F Natural Minor

F Phrygian
Natural Minor with ♭2

F Locrian
Natural Minor with ♭2 and ♭5

Bb Scales & Bb Modes

Bb Major Scale
Bb-C-D-Eb-F-G-A-Bb

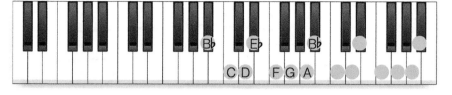

Bb Mixolydian Mode
Bb-C-D-Eb-F-G-Ab-Bb

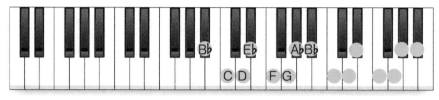

Bb Lydian Mode
Bb-C-D-E-F-G-A-Bb

Bb Melodic Minor
Bb-C-Db-Eb-F-G-A-Bb

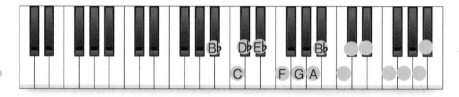

Bb Harmonic Minor
Bb-C-Db-Eb-F-Gb-A-Bb

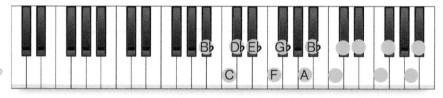

Bb Dorian Mode
Bb-C-Db-Eb-F-G-A-Bb

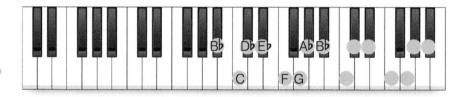

Bb Natural Minor
Bb-C-Db-Eb-F-Gb-Ab-Bb

Bb Phrygian Mode
Bb-Cb-Db-Eb-F-Gb-Ab-Bb

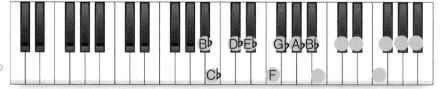

Bb Locrian Mode
Bb-Cb-Db-Eb-Fb-Gb-Ab-Bb

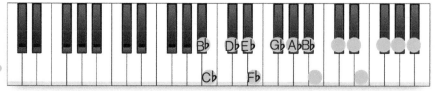

Bb Scales & Bb Modes

E♭ Scales & E♭ Modes

E♭ Major Scale
E♭-F-G-A♭-B♭-C-D-E♭

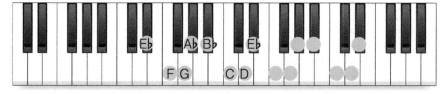

E♭ Mixolydian Mode
E♭-F-G-A♭-B♭-C-D♭-E♭

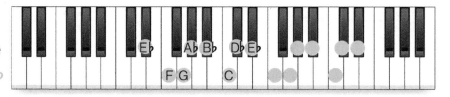

E♭ Lydian Mode
E♭-F-G-A-B♭-C-D-E♭

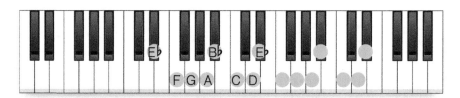

E♭ Melodic Minor
E♭-F-G♭-A♭-B♭-C-D-E♭

E♭ Harmonic Minor
E♭-F-G♭-A♭-B♭-C♭-D-E♭

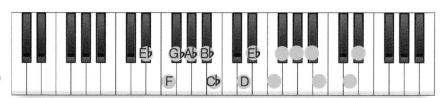

E♭ Dorian Mode
E♭-F-G♭-A♭-B♭-C-D♭-E♭

E♭ Natural Minor
E♭-F-G♭-A♭-B♭-C♭-D♭-E♭

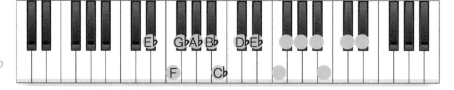

E♭ Phrygian Mode
E♭-F♭-G♭-A♭-B♭-C♭-D♭-E♭

D♯ Locrian Mode
D♯-E-F♯-G♯-A-B-C♯-D♯

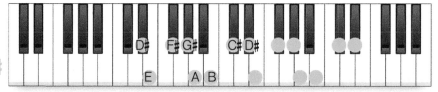

E♭ Scales & E♭ Modes

E♭ Major

E♭ Mixolydian
Major with ♭7

E♭ Lydian
Major with ♮4

E♭ Melodic Minor

E♭ Harmonic Minor

E♭ Dorian
Natural Minor with ♮6

E♭ Natural Minor

E♭ Phrygian
Natural Minor with ♭2

E♭ Locrian
Natural Minor with ♭2 and ♭♭5

Ab Scales & Ab Modes

Ab Major Scale
Ab-Bb-C-Db-Eb-F-G-Ab

Ab Mixolydian Mode
Ab-Bb-C-Db-Eb-F-Gb-Ab

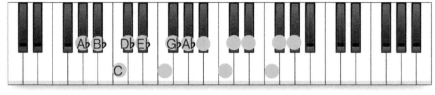

Ab Lydian Mode
Ab-Bb-C-D-Eb-F-G-Ab

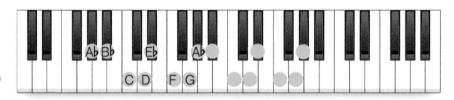

Ab Melodic Minor
Ab-Bb-Cb-Db-Eb-F-G-Ab

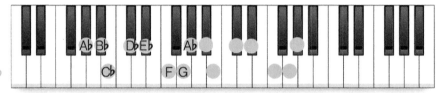

Ab Harmonic Minor
Ab-Bb-Cb-Db-Eb-Fb-G-Ab

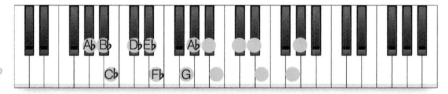

Ab Dorian Mode
Ab-Bb-Cb-Db-Eb-F-Gb-Ab

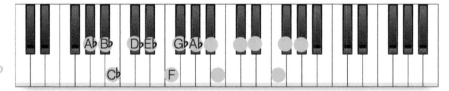

Ab Natural Minor
Ab-Bb-Cb-Db-Eb-Fb-Gb-Ab

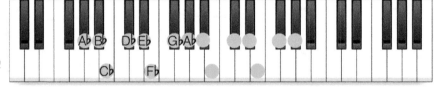

Ab Phrygian Mode
Ab-Bbb-Cb-Db-Eb-Fb-Gb-Ab

Ab Locrian Mode
Ab-Bbb-Cb-Db-Ebb-Fb-Gb-Ab

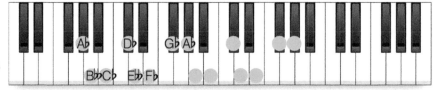

A♭ Scales & A♭ Modes

A♭ Major

A♭ Mixolydian
Major with ♭7

A♭ Lydian
Major with ♮4

A♭ Melodic Minor

A♭ Harmonic Minor

A♭ Dorian
Natural Minor with ♮6

A♭ Natural Minor

A♭ Phrygian
Natural Minor with ♭♭2

A♭ Locrian
Natural Minor with ♭♭2 and ♭♭5

D♭ Scales & D♭ Modes

D♭ Major Scale
D♭-E♭-F-G♭-A♭-B♭-C-D♭

D♭ Mixolydian Mode
D♭-E♭-F-G♭-A♭-B♭-C♭-D♭

D♭ Lydian Mode
D♭-E♭-F-G-A♭-B♭-C-D♭

C♯ Melodic Minor
C♯-D♯-E-F♯-G♯-A♯-B♯-C♯

C♯ Harmonic Minor
C♯-D♯-E-F♯-G♯-A-B♯-C♯

C♯ Dorian Mode
C♯-D♯-E-F♯-G♯-A♯-B-C♯

C♯ Natural Minor
C♯-D♯-E-F♯-G♯-A-B-C♯

C♯ Phrygian Mode
C♯-D-E-F♯-G♯-A-B-C♯

C♯ Locrian Mode
C♯-D-E-F♯-G-A-B-C♯

Db Scales & Db Modes

Db Major

Db Mixolydian
Major with b7

Db Lydian
Major with ♮4

C# Melodic Minor
Db Minor is a theoretical key. C# is the enharmonic equivalent to Db

C# Harmonic Minor

C# Dorian
Natural Minor with #6

C# Natural Minor

C# Phrygian
Natural Minor with ♮2

C# Locrian
Natural Minor with ♮2 and ♮5

Gb Scales & Gb Modes

Gb Major Scale
Gb-Ab-Bb-Cb-Db-Eb-F-Gb

Gb Mixolydian Mode
Gb-Ab-Bb-Cb-Db-Eb-Fb-Gb

Gb Lydian Mode
Gb-Ab-Bb-C-Db-Eb-F-Gb

F# Melodic Minor
F#-G#-A-B-C#-D#-E#-F#

F# Harmonic Minor
F#-G#-A-B-C#-D-E#-F#

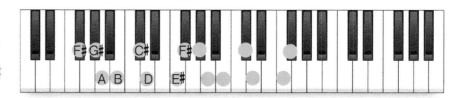

F# Dorian Mode
F#-G#-A-B-C#-D#-E-F#

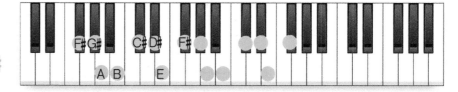

F# Natural Minor
F#-G#-A-B-C#-D-E-F#

F# Phrygian Mode
F#-G-A-B-C#-D-E-F#

F# Locrian Mode
F#-G-A-B-C-D-E-F#

G♭ Scales & G♭ Modes

G♭ Major

G♭ Mixolydian
Major with ♭7

G♭ Lydian
Major with ♮4

F# Melodic Minor
G♭ Minor is a theoretical key. F# is the enharmonic equivalent to G♭

F# Harmonic Minor

F# Dorian
Natural Minor with #6

F# Natural Minor

F# Phrygian
Natural Minor with ♮2

F# Locrian
Natural Minor with ♮2 and ♮5

46

C♭ Scales & C♭ Modes

C♭ Major Scale
C♭–D♭–E♭–F♭–G♭–A♭–B♭–C♭

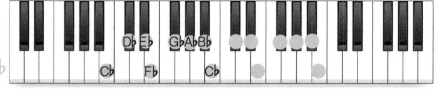

C♭ Mixolydian Mode
C♭–D♭–E♭–F♭–G♭–A♭–B♭♭–C♭

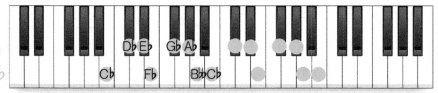

C♭ Lydian Mode
C♭–D♭–E♭–F–G♭–A♭–B♭–C♭

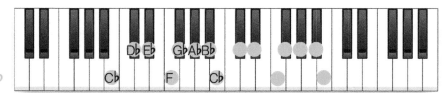

B Melodic Minor
B–C#–D–E–F#–G#–A#–B

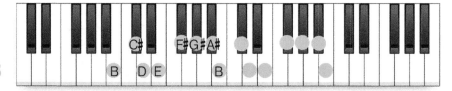

B Harmonic Minor
B–C#–D–E–F#–G–A–B

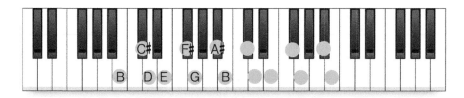

B Dorian Mode
B–C#–D–E–F#–G#–A–B

B Natural Minor
B–C#–D–E–F#–G–A–B

B Phrygian Mode
B–C–D–E–F#–G–A–B

B Locrian Mode
B–C–D–E–F–G–A–B

Cb Scales & Cb Modes

Cb Major

B Mixolydian
Major with ♮7

Cb Lydian
Major with ♮4

B Melodic Minor
Cb Minor is a theoretical key. B is the enharmonic equivalent to Cb

B Harmonic Minor

B Dorian
Natural Minor with #6

B Natural Minor

B Phrygian
Natural Minor with ♮2

B Locrian
Natural Minor with ♮2 and ♮5

Use this chart to strategize your practice for the most efficient study.

The following section of the book presents modes in the context of a major key.

All 15 major keys are presented as "Mode 1 - Ionian (Major)" and each full column lists the complete major scale. Each mode is a different starting point (scale degree) within the scale. Be sure to combine sets of enharmonic equivalents keys to reduce your workload: F#/Gb; C#/Db; B/Cb.

Mode 1 *Ionian* (Major)	C	G	D	A	E	B	F#	C#	F	Bb	Eb	Ab	Db	Gb	Cb
Mode 2 *Dorian*	D	A	E	B	F#	C#	G#	D#	G	C	F	Bb	Eb	Ab	Db
Mode 3 *Phrygian*	E	B	F#	C#	G#	D#	A#	E#	A	D	G	C	F	Bb	Eb
Mode 4 *Lydian*	F	C	G	D	A	E	B	F#	Bb	Eb	Ab	Db	Gb	Cb	Fb
Mode 5 *Mixolydian*	G	D	A	E	B	F#	C#	G#	C	F	Bb	Eb	Ab	Db	Gb
Mode 6 *Aeolian* (natural minor)	A	E	B	F#	C#	G#	D#	A#	D	G	C	F	Bb	Eb	Ab
Mode 7 *Locrian*	B	F#	C#	G#	D#	A#	E#	B#	E	A	D	G	C	F	Bb

Play all scales and modes in the context of major keys, 15 keys total. Each key has 7 modes. Keep track of your progress by checking off each scale and mode. Plan to play all scales and modes in each key starting from the left column (C major) and progressing from top to bottom from Mode 1 to 7. After mastering all keys, plan to perform any scale or mode in random order. Always perform all scales and modes in both ascending and descending motion, at least one octave.

musical fluency

In addition to performing on your instrument, be able to *sing* all scales and modes on solfege, be able to *write* out in music notation (by hand), be able to identify all scales and modes by *ear*, and practice melodic *improvisation!*

My favorite SCALES

My favorite MODES

C Major Scale & Modes

Key of C major
Relative Key: A minor
Parallel Key: C minor

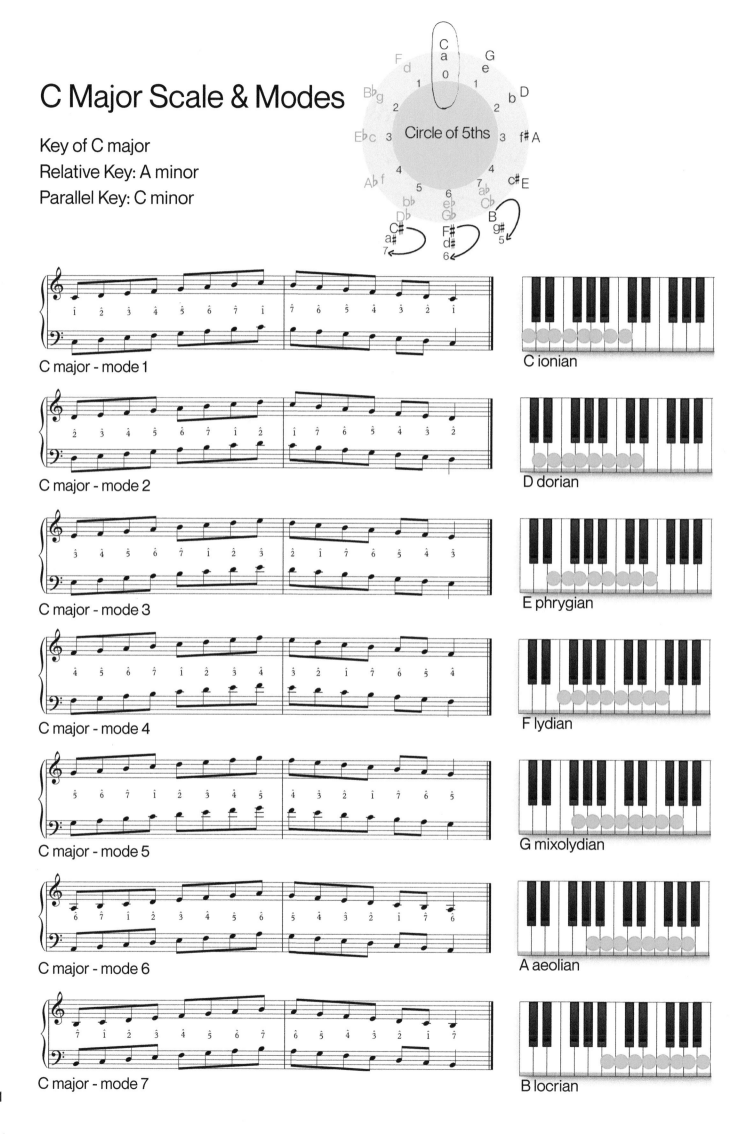

C major - mode 1 — C ionian

C major - mode 2 — D dorian

C major - mode 3 — E phrygian

C major - mode 4 — F lydian

C major - mode 5 — G mixolydian

C major - mode 6 — A aeolian

C major - mode 7 — B locrian

G Major Scale & Modes

Key of G major
Relative Key: E minor
Parallel Key: G minor

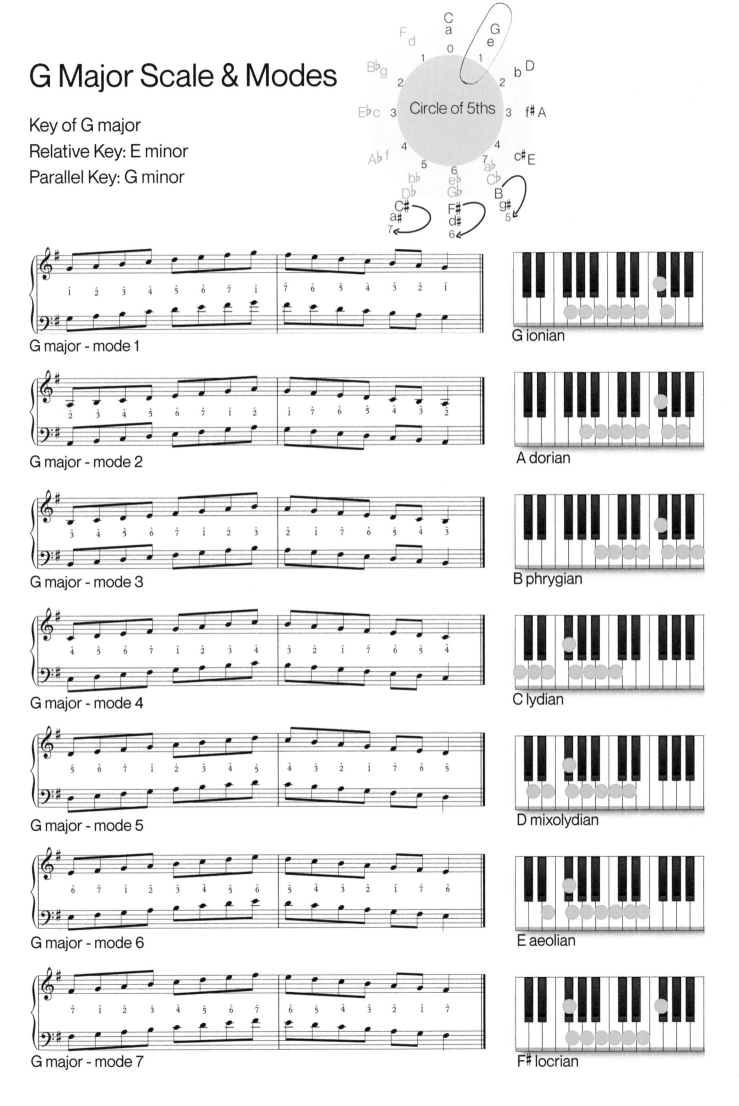

G major - mode 1

G ionian

G major - mode 2

A dorian

G major - mode 3

B phrygian

G major - mode 4

C lydian

G major - mode 5

D mixolydian

G major - mode 6

E aeolian

G major - mode 7

F# locrian

D Major Scale & Modes

Key of D major
Relative Key: B minor
Parallel Key: D minor

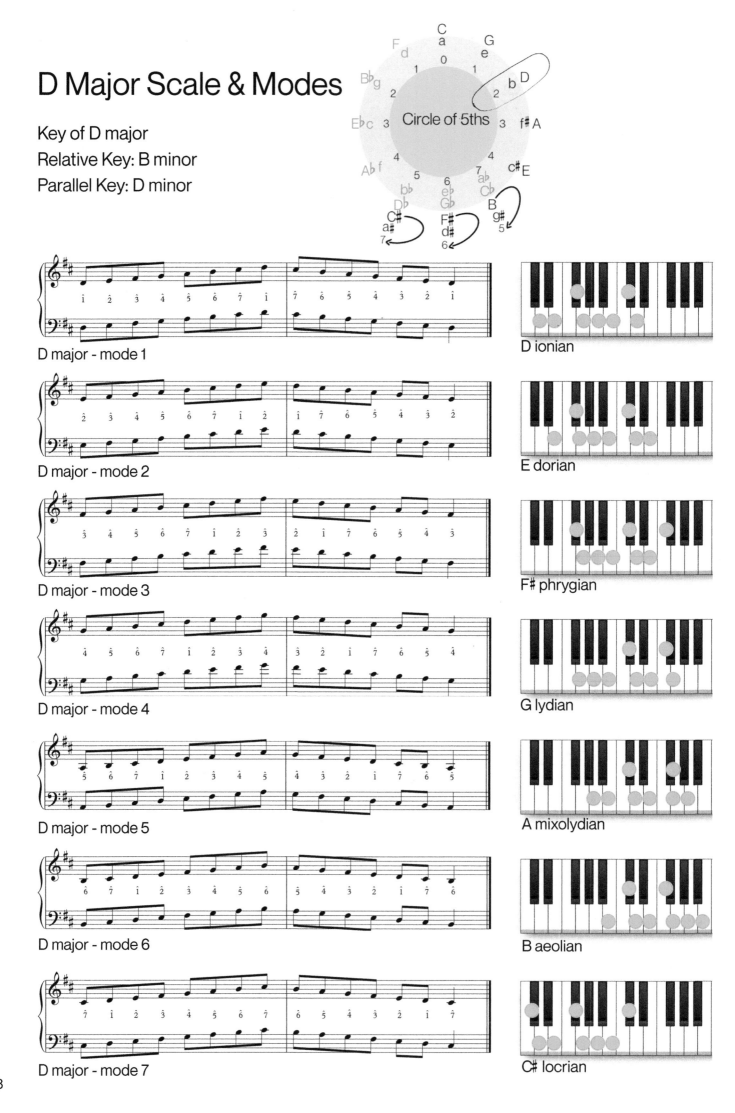

D major - mode 1 — D ionian

D major - mode 2 — E dorian

D major - mode 3 — F# phrygian

D major - mode 4 — G lydian

D major - mode 5 — A mixolydian

D major - mode 6 — B aeolian

D major - mode 7 — C# locrian

A Major Scale & Modes

Key of A major
Relative Key: F# minor
Parallel Key: A minor

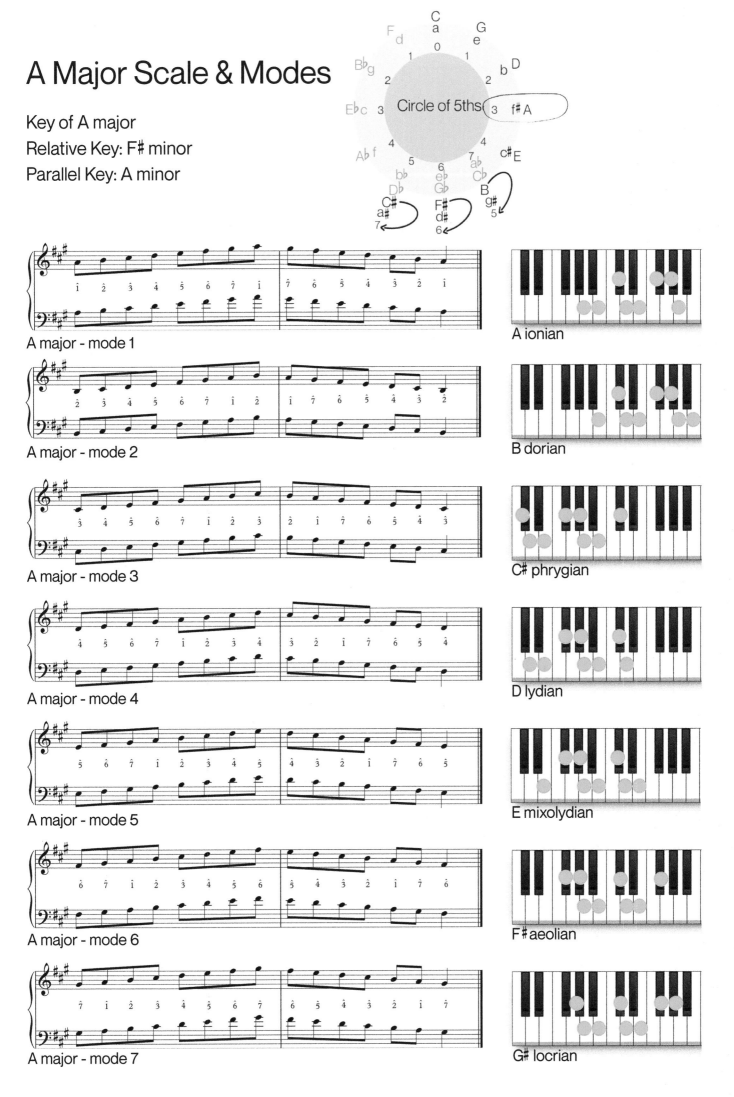

A major - mode 1 — A ionian

A major - mode 2 — B dorian

A major - mode 3 — C# phrygian

A major - mode 4 — D lydian

A major - mode 5 — E mixolydian

A major - mode 6 — F# aeolian

A major - mode 7 — G# locrian

E Major Scale & Modes

Key of E major
Relative Key: C# minor
Parallel Key: E minor

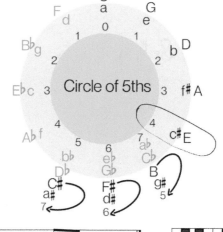
Circle of 5ths

E major - mode 1

E ionian

E major - mode 2

F# dorian

E major - mode 3

G# phrygian

E major - mode 4

A lydian

E major - mode 5

B mixolydian

E major - mode 6

C# aeolian

E major - mode 7

D# locrian

B Major Scale & Modes

Key of B major
Relative Key: G# minor
Parallel Key: B minor

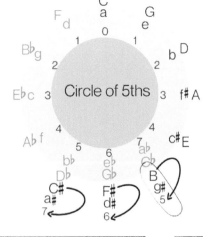

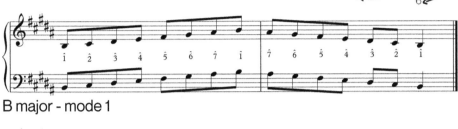

B major - mode 1

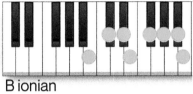

B ionian

B major - mode 2

C# dorian

B major - mode 3

D# phrygian

B major - mode 4

E lydian

B major - mode 5

F# mixolydian

B major - mode 6

G# aeolian

B major - mode 7

A# locrian

F♯ Major Scale & Modes

Key of F♯ major
Relative Key: D♯ minor
Parallel Key: F♯ minor

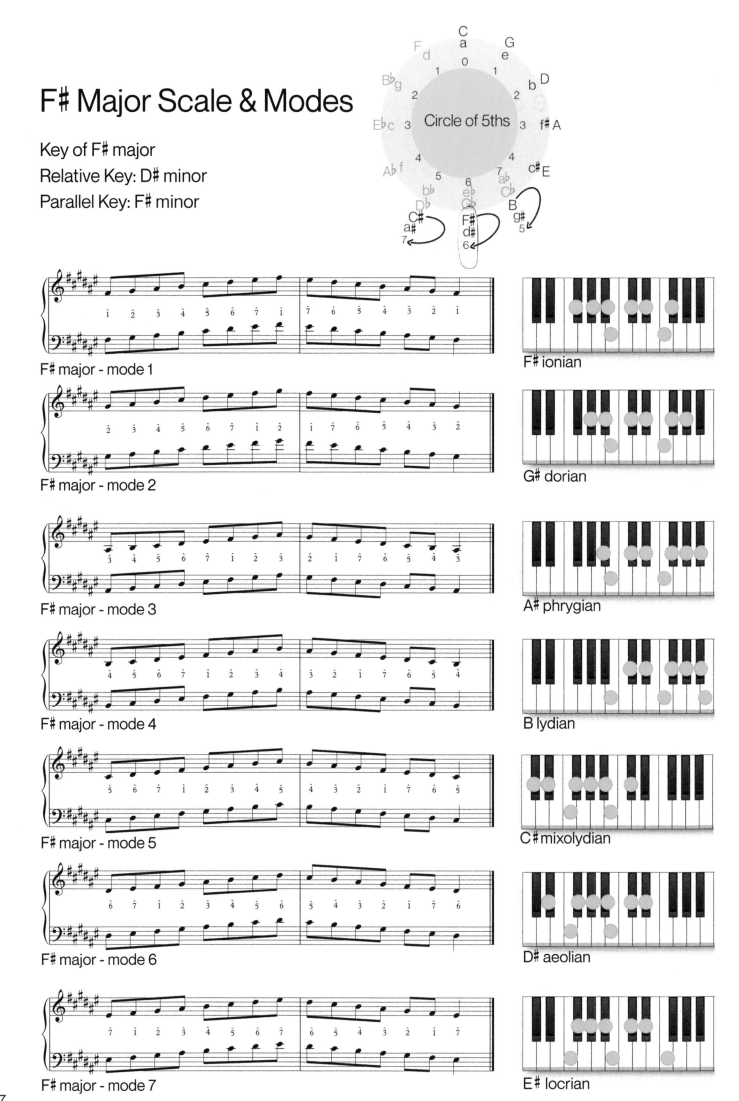

F♯ major - mode 1 — F♯ ionian

F♯ major - mode 2 — G♯ dorian

F♯ major - mode 3 — A♯ phrygian

F♯ major - mode 4 — B lydian

F♯ major - mode 5 — C♯ mixolydian

F♯ major - mode 6 — D♯ aeolian

F♯ major - mode 7 — E♯ locrian

C# Major Scale & Modes

Key of C# major
Relative Key: A# minor
Parallel Key: C# minor

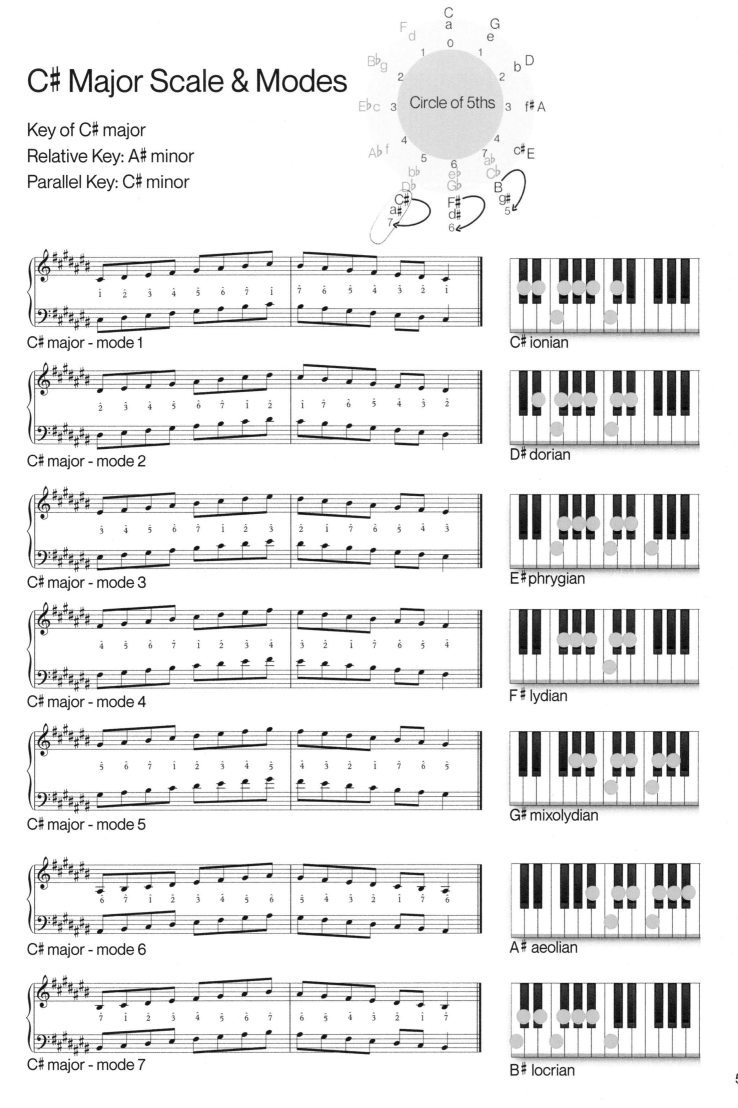

C# major - mode 1 — C# ionian

C# major - mode 2 — D# dorian

C# major - mode 3 — E# phrygian

C# major - mode 4 — F# lydian

C# major - mode 5 — G# mixolydian

C# major - mode 6 — A# aeolian

C# major - mode 7 — B# locrian

58

F Major Scale & Modes

Key of F major
Relative Key: D minor
Parallel Key: F minor

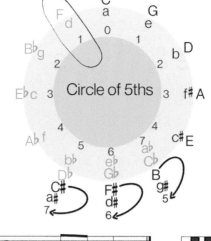

F major - mode 1

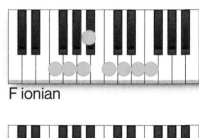

F ionian

F major - mode 2

G dorian

F major - mode 3

A phrygian

F major - mode 4

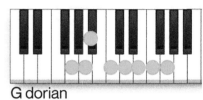

B♭ lydian

F major - mode 5

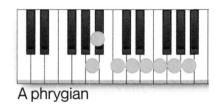

C mixolydian

F major - mode 6

D aeolian

F major - mode 7

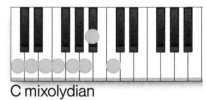

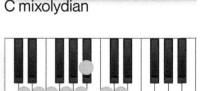

E locrian

B♭ Major Scale & Modes

Key of B♭ major
Relative Key: G minor
Parallel Key: B♭ minor

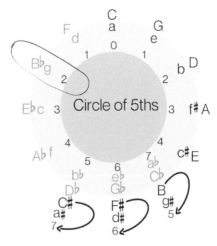

Circle of 5ths

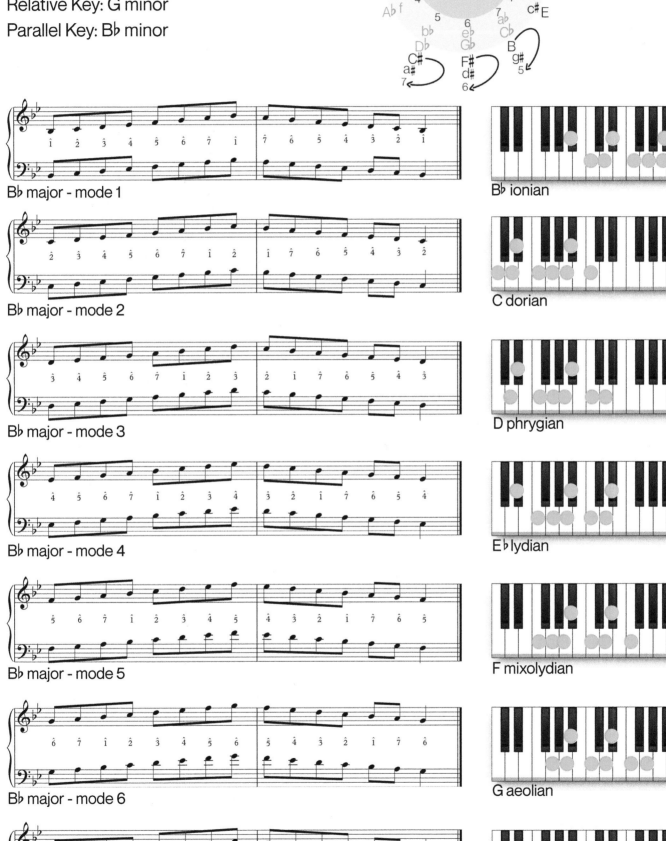

B♭ major - mode 1

B♭ ionian

B♭ major - mode 2

C dorian

B♭ major - mode 3

D phrygian

B♭ major - mode 4

E♭ lydian

B♭ major - mode 5

F mixolydian

B♭ major - mode 6

G aeolian

B♭ major - mode 7

A locrian

E♭ Major Scale & Modes

Key of E♭ major
Relative Key: C minor
Parallel Key: E♭ minor

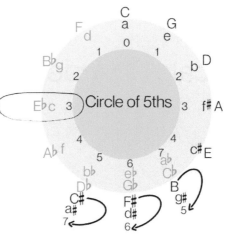

Circle of 5ths

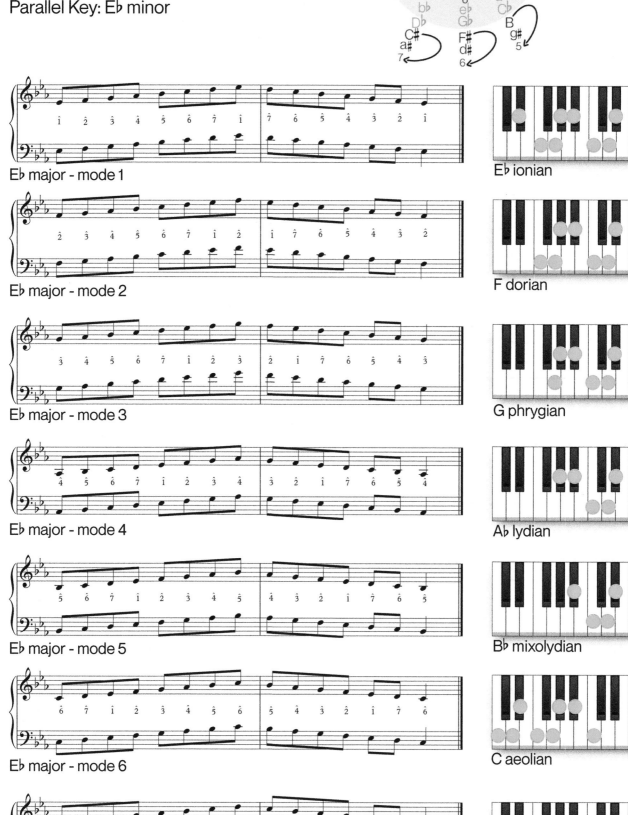

E♭ major - mode 1

E♭ ionian

E♭ major - mode 2

F dorian

E♭ major - mode 3

G phrygian

E♭ major - mode 4

A♭ lydian

E♭ major - mode 5

B♭ mixolydian

E♭ major - mode 6

C aeolian

E♭ major - mode 7

D locrian

A♭ Major Scale & Modes

Key of A♭ major
Relative Key: F minor
Parallel Key: A♭ minor

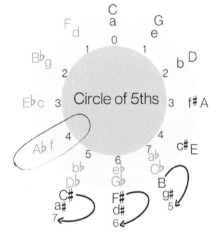

A♭ major - mode 1

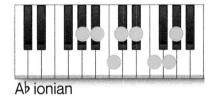

A♭ ionian

A♭ major - mode 2

B♭ dorian

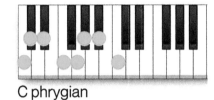

A♭ major - mode 3

C phrygian

A♭ major - mode 4

D♭ lydian

A♭ major - mode 5

E♭ mixolydian

A♭ major - mode 6

F aeolian

A♭ major - mode 7

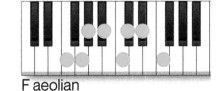

G locrian

D♭ Major Scale & Modes

Key of D♭ major
Relative Key: B♭ minor
Parallel Key: C# minor

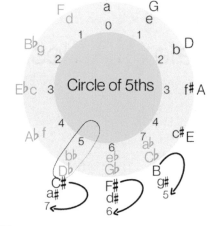

D♭ major - mode 1

D♭ major - mode 2

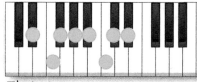
D♭ ionian

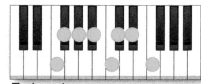

D♭ major - mode 3

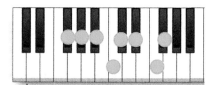
E♭ dorian

D♭ major - mode 4

F phrygian

D♭ major - mode 5

G♭ lydian

D♭ major - mode 6

A♭ mixolydian

D♭ major - mode 7

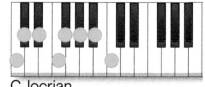
B♭ aeolian

C locrian

G♭ Major Scale & Modes

Key of G♭ major
Relative Key: E♭ minor
Parallel Key: F♯ minor

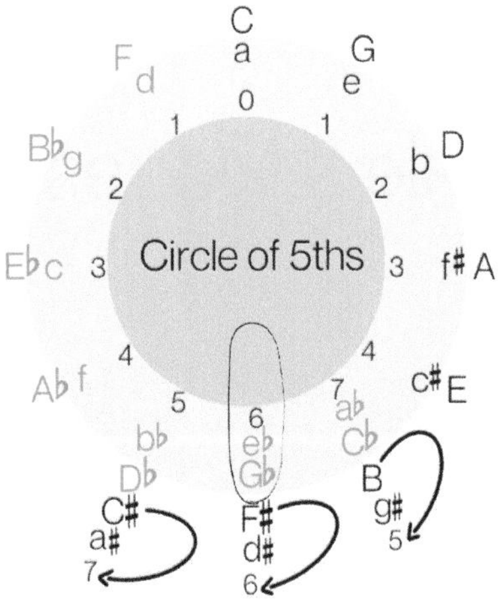

Circle of 5ths

G♭ major - mode 1

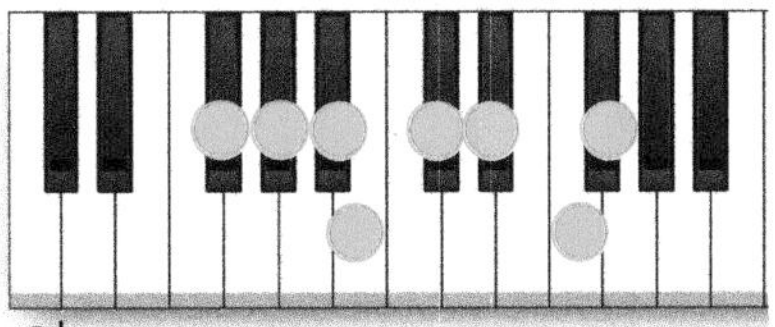

G♭ ionian

G♭ major - mode 2

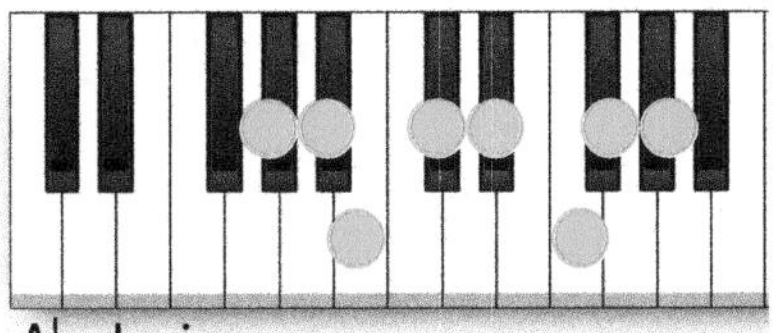

A♭ dorian

G♭ major - mode 3

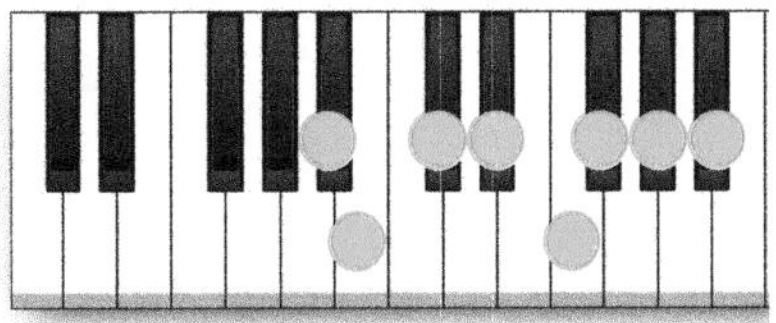

B♭ phrygian

G♭ major - mode 4

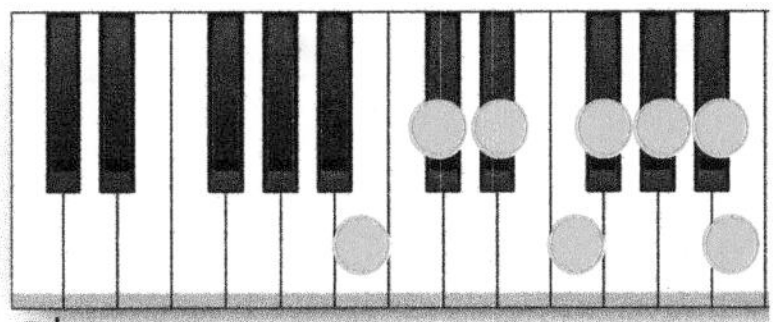

C♭ lydian

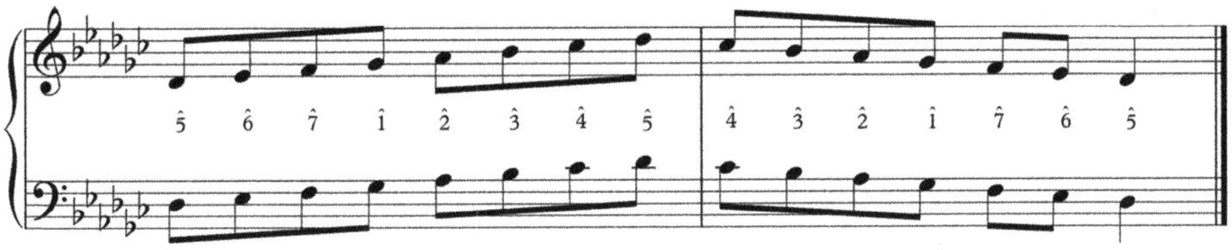

G♭ major - mode 5

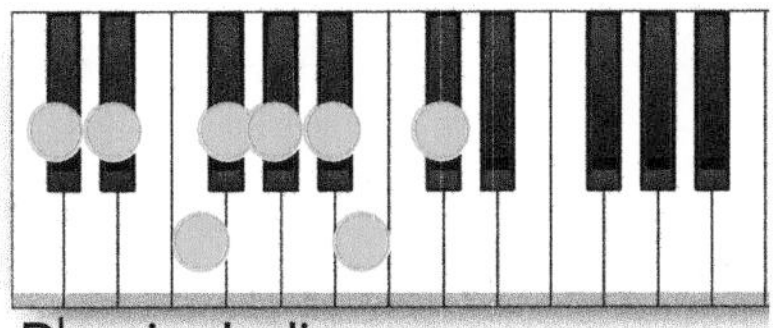

D♭ mixolydian

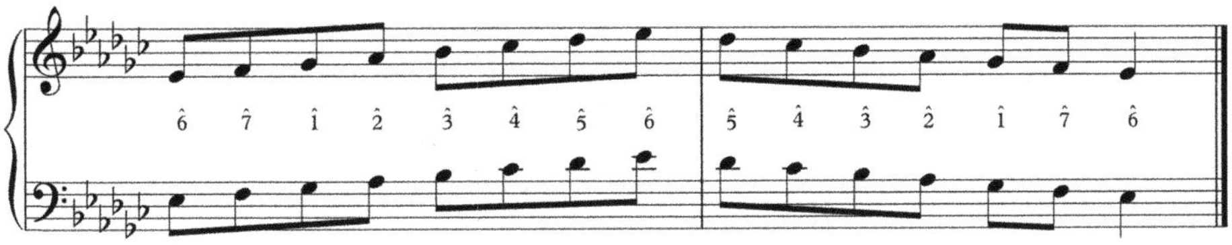

G♭ major - mode 6

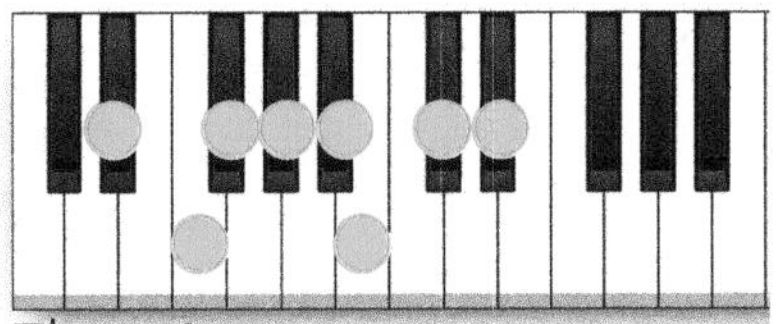

E♭ aeolian

G♭ major - mode 7

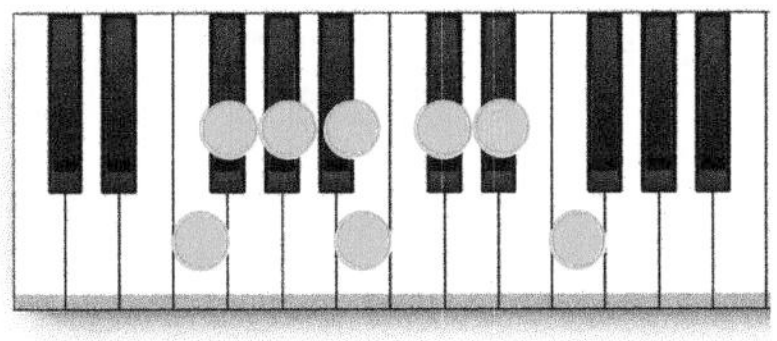

F locrian

Cb Major Scale & Modes

Key of Cb major

Relative Key: Ab minor

Parallel Key: B minor

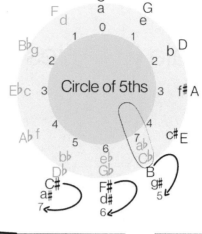

Circle of 5ths

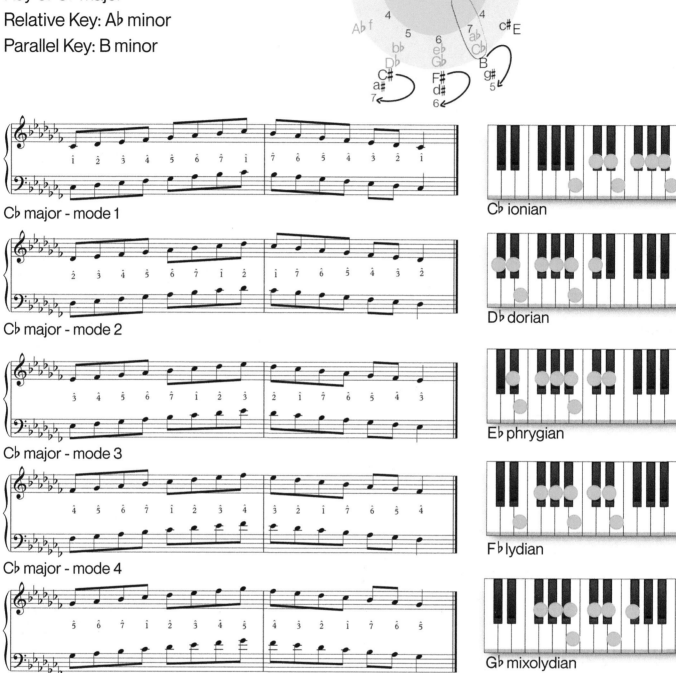

Cb major - mode 1

Cb ionian

Cb major - mode 2

Db dorian

Cb major - mode 3

Eb phrygian

Cb major - mode 4

Fb lydian

Cb major - mode 5

Gb mixolydian

Cb major - mode 6

Ab aeolian

Cb major - mode 7

Bb locrian